MATHEMATICS

Louise Moore
Series Editor: **Richard Cooper**

Rising Stars UK Ltd., 22 Grafton Street, London W1S 4EX

www.risingstars-uk.com

All facts are correct at time of going to press.

First published 2003
This edition 2008

First edition written by: Richard Cooper
Educational consultant: Allison Toogood
Project management: Cambridge Publishing Management Ltd.
Project editor: Catherine Burch
Illustrations: Tim Oliver and Clive Wakfer
Design: Neil Adcock
Cover design: Burville-Riley Partnership

British Library Cataloguing in Publication Data
A CIP record for this book is available from the British Library.

ISBN 978-1-84680-285-0

Printed by Craft Print International Ltd, Singapore

Contents

How to use this book

What we have included:

★ Those topics at Level 3 that are trickiest to get right.

★ ALL Level 4 content so you know that you are covering all the topics that could come up in the test.

★ We have also put in a big selection of our favourite test techniques, tips for revision and some advice on what the tests are all about, as well as the answers so you can see how well you are getting on.

GOOD LUCK!

(1) Introduction – This section tells you what you need to do to get a Level 4. It picks out the key learning objective and explains it simply to you.

(2) Self-assessment – Tick the face that best describes your understanding of this concept.

(3) Question – The question helps you to learn by doing. It is presented in a similar way to a National Test question and gives you a real example to work with.

(4) Flow chart – This shows you the steps to use when completing questions like this. Some of the advice appears on every flow chart (e.g. 'Read the question then read it again'). This is because this is the best way of getting good marks in the test.

(5) Tip boxes – These provide test hints and general tips on getting the best marks in the National Tests.

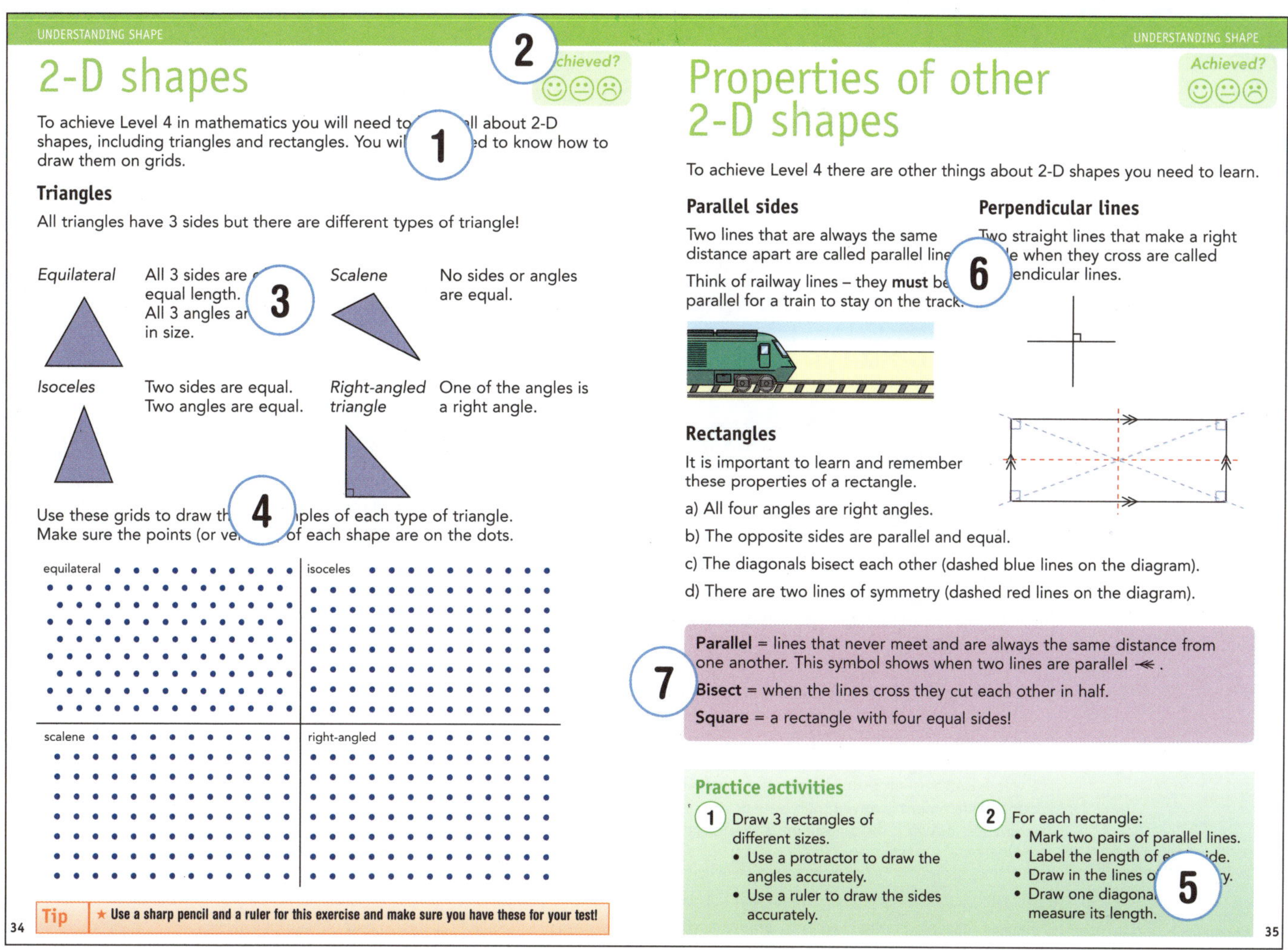

6 **Second question** – On most pages there will be a second question. This will either look at a slightly different question type or give you another example to work through.

7 **Practice questions** – This is where you have to do the work! Try the question using the technique in the flow chart then check your answers at the back. Practising questions is the best way to help improve your understanding.

Learning objectives for primary mathematics

This table may be useful for your teacher or carer. They can see what you have learnt in Year 5 and what you will be learning in Year 6. They will be able to see your progression for each strand following the Primary Mathematics Framework.

The key objectives are in **bold type**.

Strand	Year 5	Year 6
Using and applying mathematics	Solve one-step and two-step problems involving whole numbers and decimals and all four operations, choosing and using appropriate calculation strategies, including calculator use	Solve multi-step problems, and problems involving fractions, decimals and percentages; choose and use appropriate calculation strategies at each stage, including calculator use
	Represent a puzzle or problem by identifying and recording the information or calculations needed to solve it; find possible solutions and confirm them in the context of the problem	Tabulate systematically the information in a problem or puzzle; identify and record the steps or calculations needed to solve it, using symbols where appropriate; interpret solutions in the original context and check their accuracy
	Plan and pursue an enquiry; present evidence by collecting, organising and interpreting information; suggest extensions to the enquiry	Suggest, plan and develop lines of enquiry; collect, organise and represent information, interpret results and review methods; identify and answer related questions
	Explore patterns, properties and relationships and propose a general statement involving numbers or shapes; identify examples for which the statement is true or false	Represent and interpret sequences, patterns and relationships involving numbers and shapes; suggest and test hypotheses; construct and use simple expressions and formulae in words then symbols (e.g. the cost of c pens at 15 pence each is 15c pence)
	Explain reasoning using diagrams, graphs and text; refine ways of recording using images and symbols	Explain reasoning and conclusions, using words, symbols or diagrams as appropriate
Counting and understanding number	Count from any given number in whole-number and decimal steps, extending beyond zero when counting backwards; relate the numbers to their position on a number line	Find the difference between a positive and a negative integer, or two negative integers, in context
	Explain what each digit represents in whole numbers and decimals with up to two places, and partition, round and order these numbers	Use decimal notation for tenths, hundredths and thousandths; partition, round and order decimals with up to three places, and position them on the number line
	Express a smaller whole number as a fraction of a larger one (e.g. recognise that 5 out of 8 is ⅝); find equivalent fractions (e.g. ⁷⁄₁₀ = ¹⁴⁄₂₀, or ¹⁹⁄₁₀ = 1⁹⁄₁₀); relate fractions to their decimal representations	Express a larger whole number as a fraction of a smaller one (e.g. recognise that 8 slices of a 5-slice pizza represents ⁸⁄₅ or 1⅗ pizzas); simplify fractions by cancelling common factors; order a set of fractions by converting them to fractions with a common denominator
	Understand percentage as the number of parts in every 100 and express tenths and hundredths as percentages	**Express one quantity as a percentage of another (e.g. express £400 as a percentage of £1000); find equivalent percentages, decimals and fractions**
	Use sequences to scale numbers up or down; solve problems involving proportions of quantities (e.g. decrease quantities in a recipe designed to feed six people)	Solve simple problems involving direct proportion by scaling quantities up or down
Knowing and using number facts	**Use knowledge of place value and addition and subtraction of two-digit numbers to derive sums and differences and doubles and halves of decimals (e.g. 6.5 ± 2.7, half of 5.6, double 0.34)**	**Use knowledge of place value and multiplication facts to 10 × 10 to derive related multiplication and division facts involving decimals (e.g. 0.8 × 7, 4.8 ÷ 6)**
	Recall quickly multiplication facts up to 10 × 10 and use them to multiply pairs of multiples of 10 and 100; derive quickly corresponding division facts	Use knowledge of multiplication facts to derive quickly squares of numbers to 12 × 12 and the corresponding squares of multiples of 10
	Identify pairs of factors of two-digit whole numbers and find common multiples (e.g. for 6 and 9)	Recognise that prime numbers have only two factors and identify prime numbers less than 100; find the prime factors of two-digit numbers
	Use knowledge of rounding, place value, number facts and inverse operations to estimate and check calculations	Use approximations, inverse operations and tests of divisibility to estimate and check results

Strand	Year 5	Year 6
Calculating	Extend mental methods for whole-number calculations, for example to multiply a two-digit by a one-digit number (e.g. 12 × 9), to multiply by 25 (e.g. 16 × 25), to subtract one near multiple of 1000 from another (e.g. 6070 – 4097)	Calculate mentally with integers and decimals: U.t ± U.t, TU × U, TU ÷ U, U.t × U, U.t ÷ U
	Use efficient written methods to add and subtract whole numbers and decimals with up to two places	**Use efficient written methods to add and subtract integers and decimals, to multiply and divide integers and decimals by a one-digit integer, and to multiply two-digit and three-digit integers by a two-digit integer**
	Use understanding of place value to multiply and divide whole numbers and decimals by 10, 100 or 1000	Relate fractions to multiplication and division (e.g. 6 ÷ 2 = ½ of 6 = 6 × ½); express a quotient as a fraction or decimal (e.g. 67 ÷ 5 = 13.4 or 13²⁄₅); find fractions and percentages of whole-number quantities (e.g. ⅝ of 96, 65% of £260)
	Refine and use efficient written methods to multiply and divide HTU × U, TU × TU, U.t × U and HTU ÷ U	Use a calculator to solve problems involving multi-step calculations
	Find fractions using division (e.g. ¹⁄₁₀₀ of 5 kg), and percentages of numbers and quantities (e.g. 10%, 5% and 15% of £80)	
	Use a calculator to solve problems, including those involving decimals or fractions (e.g. find ¾ of 150 g); interpret the display correctly in the context of measurement	
Understanding shape	Identify, visualise and describe properties of rectangles, triangles, regular polygons and 3-D solids; use knowledge of properties to draw 2-D shapes, and to identify and draw nets of 3-D shapes	Describe, identify and visualise parallel and perpendicular edges or faces; use these properties to classify 2-D shapes and 3-D solids
	Read and plot coordinates in the first quadrant; recognise parallel and perpendicular lines in grids and shapes; use a set-square and ruler to draw shapes with perpendicular or parallel sides	Make and draw shapes with increasing accuracy and apply knowledge of their properties
	Complete patterns with up to two lines of symmetry; draw the position of a shape after a reflection or translation	**Visualise and draw on grids of different types where a shape will be after reflection, after translation, or after rotation through 90° or 180° about its centre or one of its vertices**
	Estimate, draw and measure acute and obtuse angles using an angle measurer or protractor to a suitable degree of accuracy; calculate angles in a straight line	Use coordinates in the first quadrant to draw, locate and complete shapes that meet given properties
		Estimate angles, and use a protractor to measure and draw them, on their own and in shapes; calculate angles in a triangle or around a point
Measuring	Read, choose, use and record standard metric units to estimate and measure length, weight and capacity to a suitable degree of accuracy (e.g. the nearest centimetre); convert larger to smaller units using decimals to one place (e.g. change 2.6 kg to 2600 g)	Select and use standard metric units of measure and convert between units using decimals to two places (e.g. change 2.75 litres to 2750 ml, or vice versa)
	Interpret a reading that lies between two unnumbered divisions on a scale	Read and interpret scales on a range of measuring instruments, recognising that the measurement made is approximate and recording results to a required degree of accuracy; compare readings on different scales, for example when using different instruments
	Draw and measure lines to the nearest millimetre; measure and calculate the perimeter of regular and irregular polygons; use the formula for the area of a rectangle to calculate the rectangle's area	Calculate the perimeter and area of rectilinear shapes; estimate the area of an irregular shape by counting squares
	Read timetables and time using 24-hour clock notation; use a calendar to calculate time intervals	
Handling data	Describe the occurrence of familiar events using the language of chance or likelihood	Describe and predict outcomes from data using the language of chance or likelihood
	Answer a set of related questions by collecting, selecting and organising relevant data; draw conclusions, using ICT to present features, and identify further questions to ask	**Solve problems by collecting, selecting, processing, presenting and interpreting data, using ICT where appropriate; draw conclusions and identify further questions to ask**
	Construct frequency tables, pictograms and bar and line graphs to represent the frequencies of events and changes over time	Construct and interpret frequency tables, bar charts with grouped discrete data, and line graphs; interpret pie charts
	Find and interpret the mode of a set of data	Describe and interpret results and solutions to problems using the mode, range, median and mean

About the National Tests

Key facts

* The Key Stage 2 National Tests take place in the middle of May in Year 6. You will be tested on Maths, English and Science.

* The tests take place in your school and will be marked by examiners – not your teacher!

* You will get your results in July, two months after you take the tests.

* Individual test scores are not made public but a school's combined scores are published in what are commonly known as league tables.

The Maths National Tests

You will take three tests in Maths:

Mental Maths Test – This test will be played to you on a CD. You will have to answer the questions mentally within 5, 10 or 15 seconds. This test will take about 20 minutes.

Test A – The non-calculator test. This test requires quick answers on a test paper. You will not be able to use a calculator but should show any working you do.

Test B – This test allows you to use a calculator and includes problems that will take you longer to solve. If you do calculations on the calculator, remember to write down what you did. You might get a mark for the correct method, even if you get the answer wrong. Remember, the calculator is only as good as the person who uses it!

DON'T FORGET!

Using and applying mathematics – There will be more questions testing how you use and apply your mathematical knowledge in different situations. This includes:
* knowing which is the important information in the questions
* how to check your results
* describing things mathematically using common symbols and diagrams
* explaining your reasons for conclusions that you make.

Many of the questions include elements of Using and applying mathematics but we have also added extra pages with specific questions designed to help you succeed in this new area of testing (pages 52–59).

You might be asked to explain your answers and also write possible answers. Remember, always show your method.

Test techniques

Before the test

1. When you revise, try revising a 'little and often' rather than in long sessions.

2. Learn your multiplication facts up to 10×10 so that you can recall them instantly. These are your tools for performing your calculations.

3. Revise with a friend. You can encourage and learn from each other.

4. Get a good night's sleep the night before.

5. Be prepared – bring your own pens and pencils.

During the test

1. Don't rush the first few questions. These tend to be quite straightforward, so don't make any silly mistakes.

2. READ THE QUESTION THEN READ IT AGAIN.

3. If you get stuck, don't linger on the same question – move on! You can come back to it later.

4. Never leave a multiple choice question. Make an educated guess if you really can't work out the answer.

5. Check to see how many marks a question is worth. Have you 'earned' those marks with your answer?

6. Check your answers. You can use the inverse method or the rounding method. Does your answer look correct?

7. Be aware of the time. After 20 minutes, check to see how far you have got.

8. Try to leave a couple of minutes at the end to check through what you have written.

9. Always show your method. You may get a mark for showing you have gone through the correct procedure even if your answer is wrong.

10. Don't leave any questions unanswered. In the two minutes you have left yourself at the end, make an educated guess at the questions you really couldn't do.

Number problems

When you solve word problems at Level 4, you need to work out whether to add, subtract, multiply or divide.

Let's practise!

1. Read the question then read it again.

2. Write down the numbers.

4   8

3. Decide which operation to use and calculate.

'every day for 8 days.'
That means multiply, so $4 \times 8 = 32$.

4. Check the question – is your answer sensible?

32 pages is a sensible answer.

If you have to do a division sum in a number problem, you might need to round the answer up or down.

1. Read the question then read it again.

2. Write down the numbers.

5   37

3. Decide which operation to use and calculate.

'How many boxes can he fill?'
It's division. $37 \div 5 = 7\ r2$

4. Round up or down?

He can't fill 8 boxes, so the answer is 7.

Decimal notation and negative numbers

Money

We use 'decimal notation' to record money, using pounds and pence.
A penny is one hundredth of a pound.

Five pounds forty-two is written like this:

Before the decimal point is the number of whole pounds.

After the decimal point is the fraction of a pound (or number of pence).

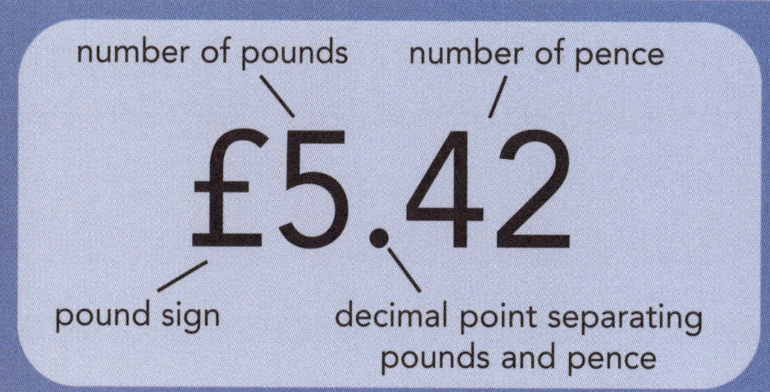

For each of these amounts, write the number of pounds and number of pence:

1 £8.26   **2** £56.40   **3** £28.04   **4** £780.75   **5** £712.97

| pounds | pounds | pounds | pounds | pounds |
| pence | pence | pence | pence | pence |

Tip ★ When writing money ALWAYS put two digits after the decimal point.
For example: £3 and 5p = £3.05 (not £3.5 or £3.50)
£7 and 40p = £7.40 (not £7.4 or £7.04)

Temperature

Negative numbers are numbers below zero. Thermometers measure temperature and use numbers below zero when it is freezing (0°C).

a) 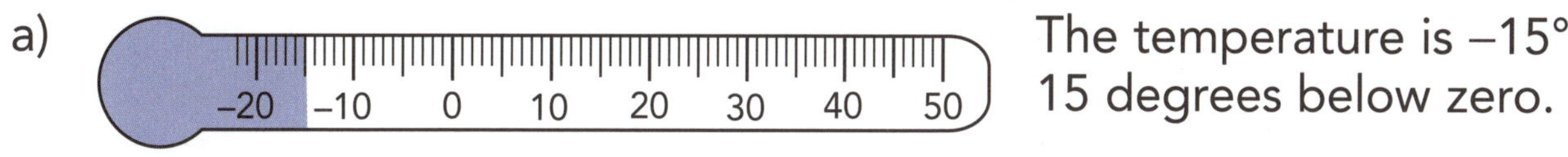

The temperature is −15°C or 15 degrees below zero.

b) 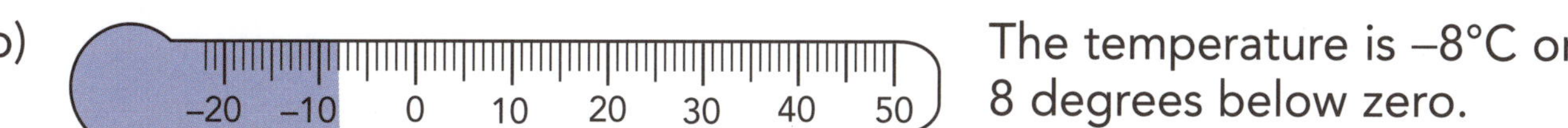

The temperature is −8°C or 8 degrees below zero.

Which do you think is colder?   a) ⬜   b) ⬜

Tip ★ Don't forget to include zero when counting up and down a temperature scale.
Think of a thermometer like a number line.
The greater the negative number on a thermometer, the colder it is.

Fractions

To achieve Level 4 you need to use fractions and recognise when two fractions are equivalent.

A fraction is part of a 'whole number'.

A quarter or $\frac{1}{4}$ means 1 part out of 4 equal parts. One quarter of this diagram has been shaded.

Three quarters or $\frac{3}{4}$ means 3 parts out of 4 equal parts. Three quarters of this diagram has **not** been shaded.

Have a look at the groups of marbles.

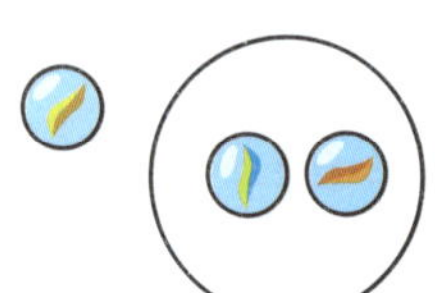

What fraction is circled?

What fraction is not circled?

Answer $\frac{2}{3}$ or two thirds.

Answer $\frac{1}{3}$ or one third.

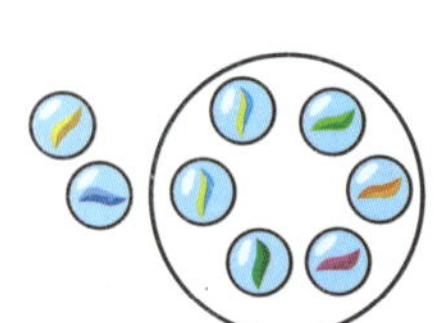

Try these questions.

What fraction is circled?

What fraction is not circled?

Equivalent fractions

Equivalent fractions are worth the same, even though they look different.

Eating $\frac{2}{4}$ of a cake is **the same as** or **equivalent** to eating $\frac{1}{2}$ a cake.

Look at this chart of equivalent fractions.

Look at one half ($\frac{1}{2}$). Can you see it is equivalent to (the same as): $\frac{2}{4}$, $\frac{3}{6}$ and $\frac{4}{8}$?

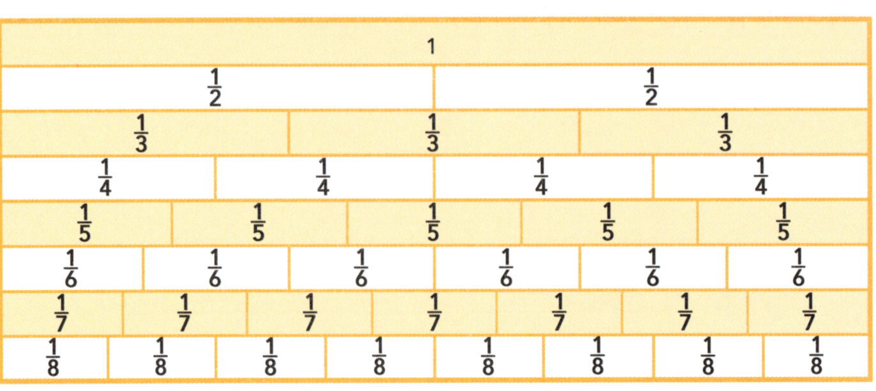

Study the chart to find more equivalent fractions. Write two here:

[ ] is the same as [ ]   [ ] is the same as [ ]

2, 3, 4, 5 and 10 times tables

Achieved? 

To achieve Level 4 you will need to know and be able to use all these table facts.

2 times table	3 times table	4 times table	5 times table	10 times table
$1 \times 2 = 2$	$1 \times 3 = 3$	$1 \times 4 = 4$	$1 \times 5 = 5$	$1 \times 10 = 10$
$2 \times 2 = 4$	$2 \times 3 = 6$	$2 \times 4 = 8$	$2 \times 5 = 10$	$2 \times 10 = 20$
$3 \times 2 = 6$	$3 \times 3 = 9$	$3 \times 4 = 12$	$3 \times 5 = 15$	$3 \times 10 = 30$
$4 \times 2 = 8$	$4 \times 3 = 12$	$4 \times 4 = 16$	$4 \times 5 = 20$	$4 \times 10 = 40$
$5 \times 2 = 10$	$5 \times 3 = 15$	$5 \times 4 = 20$	$5 \times 5 = 25$	$5 \times 10 = 50$
$6 \times 2 = 12$	$6 \times 3 = 18$	$6 \times 4 = 24$	$6 \times 5 = 30$	$6 \times 10 = 60$
$7 \times 2 = 14$	$7 \times 3 = 21$	$7 \times 4 = 28$	$7 \times 5 = 35$	$7 \times 10 = 70$
$8 \times 2 = 16$	$8 \times 3 = 24$	$8 \times 4 = 32$	$8 \times 5 = 40$	$8 \times 10 = 80$
$9 \times 2 = 18$	$9 \times 3 = 27$	$9 \times 4 = 36$	$9 \times 5 = 45$	$9 \times 10 = 90$
$10 \times 2 = 20$	$10 \times 3 = 30$	$10 \times 4 = 40$	$10 \times 5 = 50$	$10 \times 10 = 100$

Tip 1 ★ Answers are always even numbers.

Tip 2 ★ The digits, when added together, make 3, 6 or 9.

Tip 3 ★ The answers are double the 2 times table.

Tip 4 ★ The answers always end in 5 or 0.

Tip 5 ★ The answers always end in 0.

Using tables facts to help with division sums

Remember, division is the inverse or opposite of multiplication.

Example: $5 \times 4 = 20$ so $20 \div 4 = 5$

Practice questions

Use the multiplication tables to complete these division facts.

1. $12 \div 6 = \boxed{}$

2. $28 \div 4 = \boxed{}$

3. $\boxed{} \div 7 = 10$

4. $36 \div 4 = \boxed{}$

5. $25 \div \boxed{} = 5$

6. $\boxed{} \div 2 = 7$

7. $16 \div \boxed{} = 2$

8. $\boxed{} \div 10 = 8$

9. $36 \div 6 = \boxed{}$

10. $\boxed{} \div 4 = 8$

11. $40 \div \boxed{} = 8$

12. $20 \div 4 = \boxed{}$

13. $\boxed{} \div 2 = 3$

14. $4 \div 4 = \boxed{}$

15. $21 \div 3 = \boxed{}$

Subtraction

Written subtractions

To achieve Level 4 you need to be able to solve subtractions that are too hard to do in your head.

Let's practise!

1   Estimate first.   **850 – 500. The answer will be around 350.**

2   Write the digits neatly in their columns.

```
  H  T  U
  8  3  8
- 4  8  7
_________
```

3   Subtract the units, then the tens. If the top number is smaller than the bottom number, exchange across from the next column.

```
   H   T  U
  7 8 13  8
 -  4  8  7
___________
        5  1
```

In the tens column, 3 is smaller than 8 so we need to exchange from the hundreds column. 13 – 8 = 5

4   Now subtract the hundreds.

```
   H   T  U
  7 8 13  8
 -  4  8  7
___________
   3  5  1
```

5   Does your answer look sensible?   **Yes, the estimate was 350.**

Practice questions

Try these. Estimate your answer first.

1   573 – 264 =   **2**   645 – 263 =   **3**   547 – 288 =

4   740 – 423 =   **5**   590 – 326 =   **6**   840 – 479 =

Tips	★ Work step by step, starting with the units and working across the sum.	★ Remember that you can check the answer to a subtraction by using addition.

Classifying shapes

3-D (three-dimensional) shapes

To achieve Level 4, you need to be able to describe 3-D shapes using the correct words.

3-D shapes are solid shapes. They are made up of faces, edges and vertices.

- A face is a flat surface of a solid shape.

- An edge is where two faces meet.

- A vertex is a corner.

When looking at pictures of 3-D shapes you have to imagine the bits you can't see.

This picture of a cube shows 3 faces but, of course, there are actually 6!

Complete this chart. Try to picture the shapes in your mind.

	Cone	Cylinder	Sphere	Cuboid	Triangular-based pyramid	Triangular prism
Number of faces						
Number of edges						
Number of vertices						

2-D (two-dimensional) shapes

2-D shapes are 'flat shapes'. If they have straight sides they are called polygons. If they have straight sides and all the angles and sides are equal they are called regular polygons.

Symmetry

A shape is symmetrical (has symmetry) if both sides are the same when a mirror line is drawn. This is also called 'reflective symmetry'. Take a look:

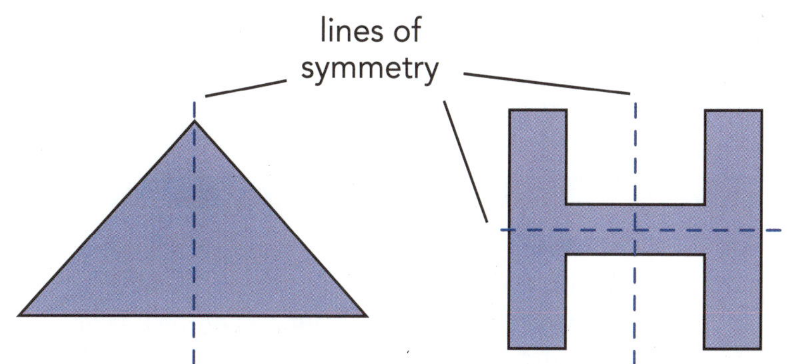

Tables and lists

The key to getting a Level 4 is to find the information you need to answer the question. This step-by-step guide will help you score maximum marks.

1 Read the question then read it again.

Make sure you understand what you are being asked to find out.

2 Check the information in the table or list.

Some tables are complicated. Always read and think carefully.

3 Use your finger or pencil to go along the rows or down the columns.

Find the information you need.

4 Read the question again and check your answer.

If your answer makes sense, write it down.

Practice questions

Here is a table about three children in a Year 3 class.

Likes playing with	Jessica	Enya	Thomas
CHAZZ! dolls	✗	✗	✓
Toy truck	✓	✓	✗
My Little T-Rex	✓	✗	✓
My dog	✗	✓	✗
Justin from Year 4	✓	✓	✓

Use the table to answer these questions:

1 Who doesn't like toy trucks?

____

2 How many children like My Little T-Rex?

____

3 Who and what do both Jessica and Thomas like to play with?

____

Tip	★ **Key words and phrases might include:** **How many …? Who …? What is …? Where can you find …?** **Which one …? When does …? When can …? What comes after …?**

Bar charts and pictograms

This step-by-step approach gives you a system so that you can read charts and graphs accurately. That's important if you want to achieve Level 4!

1 Read the information carefully.

What is the graph or chart trying to tell you?

2 On a graph, check what each axis represents.

Check the numbers going up the side (the *y* axis). Do they go up in 1s, 2s, 5s or 10s?

3 On a pictogram, check what each symbol (picture) represents.

If one symbol is worth two sandwiches, for example, what is half the symbol worth?

4 Read the question then read it again. Find the row or column with the information you need and work out the amounts using the numbers or symbols.

Use your finger or ruler to help you. ALWAYS double-check your answer.

Practice questions

Here is a bar chart showing the favourite sandwich fillings in Year 6.

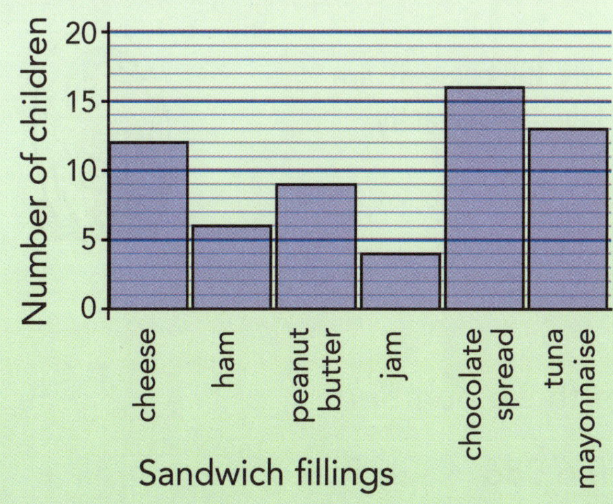

Here is the same information in a pictogram. A pictogram uses symbols to show a group of units.

cheese

ham

peanut butter

jam

chocolate spread

tuna mayonnaise

= 2 children

= 1 child

1 Which is the second most popular filling? _______________

2 How many more children like chocolate spread than peanut butter?

____

3 How many children in total like cheese and ham fillings? _______________

Place value

Achieved? ☺ 😐 ☹

To achieve Level 4 you need to understand that decimals are numbers that come in between whole numbers. Look at 3.8 on the number line. We say '3 point 8'. It has one decimal place (8 tenths). To achieve Level 4 you need to use and understand decimals with up to three decimal places: tenths, hundredths and thousandths.

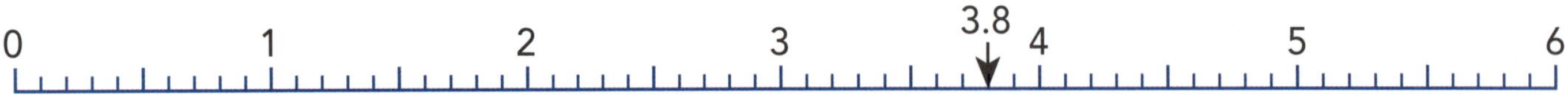

Let's practise!

What are the digits 3 and 6 worth in the number 54.673?

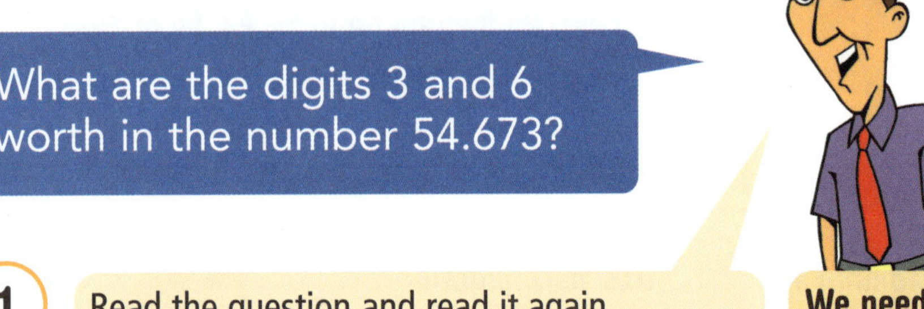

1. Read the question and read it again. — **We need to know the value of 3 and 6.**
2. Write the number. — **54.673 is in between 54 and 55.**
3. Work out what the digits stand for. — **Use**

H	T	U	.	tenths	hundredths	thousandths
	5	4	.	6	7	3

So 3 means $\frac{3}{1000}$ and 6 means $\frac{6}{10}$

4. Does your answer look sensible? If not, go back to step 3. — **Yes, the columns are labelled correctly.**

Practice questions

1. Write the value of the digit 8 in each of these numbers:

a) 56.08 b) 58.06 c) 5.608 d) 6.086 e) 856.65

2. Write the value of each digit in these numbers:

a) 3.675 b) 45.073 c) 60.007

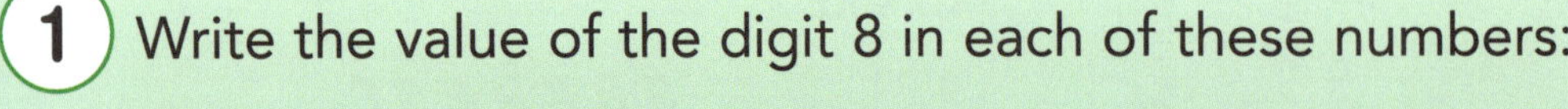

To achieve Level 4 you must show you can order decimal numbers.

Let's practise!

These are the distances jumped in the long jump competition at the school sports day by class 6C.

| Keeley 3.65 m | Jamie 3.75 m | Dominic 2.73 m |
| Ellie 3.3 m | Harry 2.79 m | Seniz 2.7 m |

Write down the distances in order of size, starting with the furthest jump.

1st __________ 2nd __________ 3rd __________
4th __________ 5th __________ 6th __________

1 Read the question and read it again.

Lots to read here. Be careful! 'Furthest' means 'highest number'.

2 List the numbers, lining up the decimal points.

3.65   Remember to put zeros in any spaces.
2.73
2.79
3.75
3.30
2.70

3 Order the numbers. Find the highest, then the next highest. Write them down.

3.75 is highest, then 3.65.

4 Continue until all the numbers are ordered.

Now 3.30, followed by 2.79. 2.73 is further than 2.70.

5 Check the order is sensible. If not, go back to step 2.

3.75, 3.65, 3.3, 2.79, 2.73, 2.7
These are in size order.

Practice questions

Put these decimals in order. Start with the **smallest** number.

1 5.68, 5.86, 58.6, 56.8, 5.66

2 8.456, 8.546, 8.654, 8.564, 8.645

3 4.7, 7.5, 7.4, 7.3, 7.9, 4.9

4 3.66 km, 36.6 km, 36.36 km, 3.36 km, 3.663 km

Proportions of a whole

To achieve Level 4 you need to be able to find a simple proportion (part) of a whole as a decimal, a fraction or a percentage.

Percentages

'Per cent' means 'out of 100'.

Let's practise!

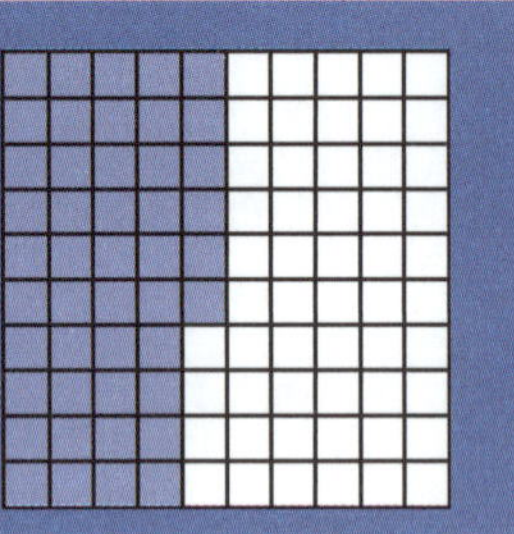

1	Read the question and read it again.	We need to find the percentage.
2	Count the squares in the grid.	There are 10 rows of 10 squares, which make 100 squares.
3	Count the number of coloured squares.	4 columns of 10 are coloured, and in another column 6 are coloured. This makes 46 squares.
4	Express the shaded amounted as part of 100.	There are 46 out of 100 coloured.
5	Express this as a percentage.	46 'out of 100' is the same as 46 per cent, so 46% is shaded.
6	Check your answer.	46% is just less than $\frac{1}{2}$, and we can see that slightly less than $\frac{1}{2}$ the shape is coloured.

Practice questions

1 What percentage of these squares is shaded?

a)  b)  c) 

2 Write the percentage of each of the above squares that is **not** shaded.

a)   b)   c)

Important proportions

Important proportions of whole objects

Parts of whole objects can be written in different ways. To achieve Level 4 you need to learn these proportions:

Halves ($\frac{1}{2}$) or 50% or 0.5

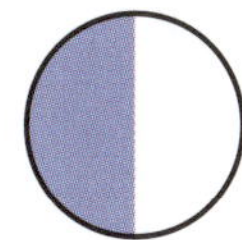 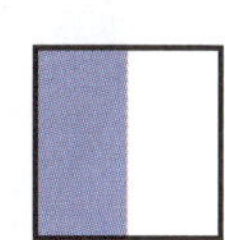   

Quarters ($\frac{1}{4}$) or 25% or 0.25

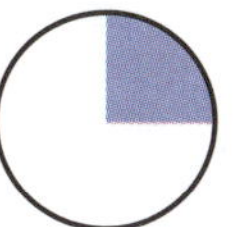    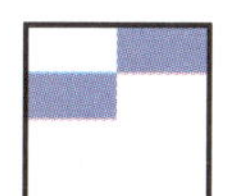

Three-quarters ($\frac{3}{4}$) or 75% or 0.75

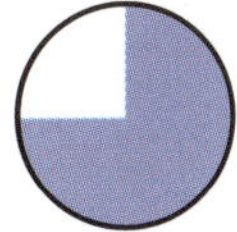 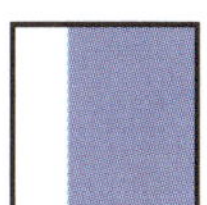  

Tenths ($\frac{1}{10}$) or 10% or 0.1

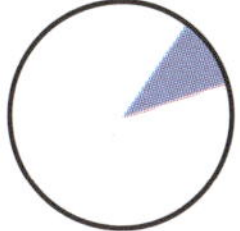   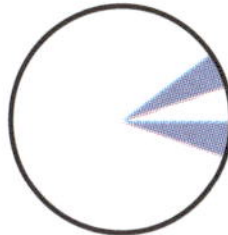

Thirds ($\frac{1}{3}$) or 33% (approx.) or 0.33 (approx.)

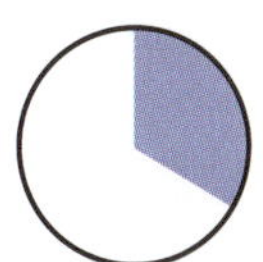  

Two-thirds or ($\frac{2}{3}$) or 66% (approx.) or 0.66 (approx.)

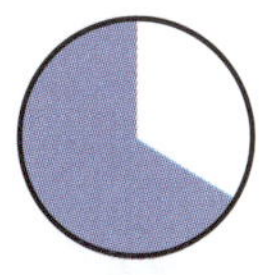  

Practice question

Try this question. You need to use what you have learnt about proportions to help you find the answers.

160 people went past school in an hour. Class A wrote down how they were travelling.

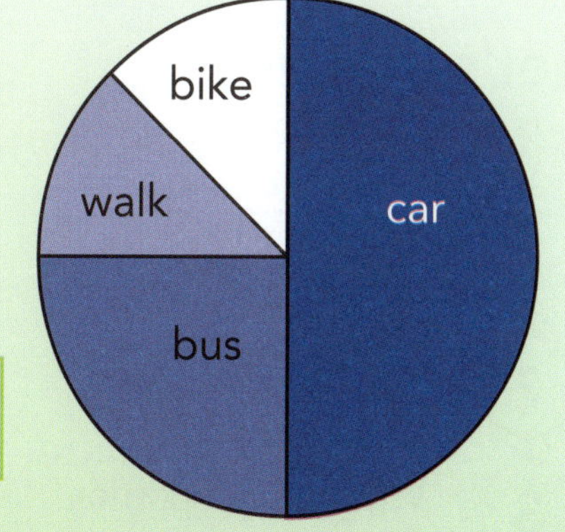

a) Which transport was chosen by 80 people?
   (Can you see the part that shows 80 out of 160? This is half of the total.)

b) How many people were travelling on the bus?
   (Can you see the shape of the number of people travelling by bus? It is a quarter.)

Ratio and proportion

To achieve Level 4 you need to know how to read and to understand the vocabulary of ratio and proportion.

Ratio

Ratio compares one part of a set to another part.

Let's practise!

1	Read the question and read it again.	We are comparing purple and orange flowers.
2	Write the numbers.	There are 7 purple and 5 orange flowers.
3	Write the ratio.	There are 7 purple flowers to 5 orange flowers. (This can be written 7:5.)
4	Check your answer.	We have counted correctly.

Proportion

Proportion compares one part of a set to the whole set.

Let's practise!

1	Read the question and read it again.	We are comparing purple flowers to the whole bunch of flowers.
2	Write the numbers.	There are 7 purple flowers and 12 flowers.
3	Write the proportion.	There are 7 purple flowers out of the 12 flowers. (This can be written $\frac{7}{12}$.)
4	Check your answer.	We have counted correctly.

Practice questions

1 What is the ratio of red sweets to green sweets?

2 What is the proportion of green sweets?

Number relationships

To achieve Level 4 you need to understand and identify factors, multiples and square numbers.

Factors

Factors are numbers that divide exactly into other numbers.

The factors of 12 are: 1, 2, 3, 4, 6 and 12.

The factors of 10 are: 1, 2, 5 and 10.

Practice questions

List all the factors of:

1 24

2 35

3 49

4 64

Square numbers

Square numbers are made when you multiply a number by itself.

Example: 4 squared is $4 \times 4 = 16$

They are called square numbers because the multiplication rows make a square. Can you find all the square numbers up to 100?

Tip	★ You need to know all the times tables up to 10 for Level 4. Knowing the square numbers helps.

Multiples

Multiples are made by multiplying one number by another. Think of multiple as **'made by multiplying by'**. So multiples of 5 are made by multiplying by 5.

Tips	★ If a number is a multiple of 2, the last digit will be even. (20, 22, 24, 26 …) ★ If a number is a multiple of 3, the sum of its digits can be divided by 3. ($57 = 5 + 7 = 12$ or $114 = 1 + 1 + 4 = 6$) ★ If a number is a multiple of 4, the last two digits can be divided by 4. (780 or 436 or 916) ★ If a number is a multiple of 5, the last digit is a 0 or a 5. (1055, 260, 475) ★ If a number is a multiple of 6, it must be an even number and the sum of its digits must be divisible by 3. ($1488 = 1 + 4 + 8 + 8 = 21$)	★ If a number is a multiple of 7, it is a tricky one and you will just have to work it out the long way. 7 is awkward, it doesn't like rules! ★ If a number is a multiple of 8, then half the number can be divided by 4. ($528 \div 2 = 264 \div 4 = 66$) ★ If a number is a multiple of 9, then the sum of its digits is divisible by 9. ($378 = 3 + 7 + 8 = 18$) ★ If a number is a multiple of 10, then the last digit is 0. (290, 1000, 2020)

Checking your answers

Checking your results should be something you do automatically when you answer a question. It can save you marks in a test and help you to become more accurate with your answers.

Here are five excellent ways you can check the results of your calculations.

Inverse operations

Remember, adding and subtracting are OPPOSITES. Multiplying and dividing are OPPOSITES. We can use this knowledge to check our answers quickly.

Example:
75 + 95 = 170   Check: 170 − 95 = 75
OR   38 × 6 = 228   Check: 228 ÷ 6 = 38

Practice questions

1. 524 − 67 = ☐   Check: ☐ + 67 = ☐

2. 160 ÷ 4 = ☐   Check: ☐ × 4 = ☐

3. 7884 − 897 = ☐   Check: ☐ + 897 = ☐

4. 2250 ÷ 50 = ☐   Check: ☐ × 50 = ☐

Approximate by rounding

Another way to check your answers is to round the numbers in the question up or down to the nearest 10, 100 or 1000. This will give you a simple sum to do first and give you a rough answer.

Example:
297 + 805 is about 300 + 800   Easy! 1100
38 × 19 is about 40 × 20   Easy! 800

You can then check your final answer against your rough answer – they should be fairly close. If not, check your rough answer and then your calculation.

Practice questions

1. 687 × 11 =   Rough answer _________________________ ☐

2. 391 − 108 =   Rough answer _________________________ ☐

3. 468 ÷ 18 =   Rough answer _________________________ ☐

Forwards and backwards

When adding several numbers together, try adding them again but backwards. It doesn't matter what order you add numbers together, the answer will be the same.

Example:
11 + 12 + 13 = 36   or   13 + 12 + 11 = 36

Try this sum, starting from the top of the units column. Now check by starting at the bottom of the units column and continuing. Were you correct?

```
    3 7 4
    5 3 6
      2 8
+     7 3
_________

```

Addition	Subtraction	Multiplication
• If you add two even numbers, your answer is even.	• If you find the difference of two even numbers, your answer is even.	• If you multiply two even numbers, your answer is even.
• If you add two odd numbers, your answer is even.	• If you find the difference of two odd numbers, your answer is even.	• If you multiply two odd numbers, your answer is odd.
• If you add one odd and one even number, your answer is odd.	• If you find the difference of one odd and one even number, your answer is odd.	• If you multiply one odd and one even number, your answer is even.

Does your answer 'look right'? (Treat your calculator with care!)

It is always worth taking a couple of seconds to redo a calculation to make sure you have pressed the right buttons.

Billy answers the question 435 × 12 on his calculator.
His calculator displays the answer 48720.

Billy looks at his answer and knows he is wrong.
He redoes the calculation and gets the answer 5220.

Billy used his knowledge of multiplication by 10 and 100 to help him.

Can you work out what Billy did wrong in his first calculation?

Addition

To achieve Level 4, you need to be able to add several numbers, including some greater than 1000.

Let's practise!

1 Read the question and read it again.

'total of' means it's an addition sum.

2 Write the numbers. Estimate an answer.

Round and estimate: 700 + 50 + 2800 = 3550

3 Write the digits in the correct columns.

```
Th H T U
   6 8 2
     5 2
 + 2 8 2 7
 ─────────
```

4 Start by adding the units.

```
Th H T U
   6 8 2
     5 2
 + 2 8 2 7
 ─────────
         1
       1
```

If the total is over 9, carry the tens digit to the next column.

5 Now work across the sum with the tens, then the hundreds, and then the thousands.

```
Th H T U
   6 8 2
     5 2
 + 2 8 2 7
 ─────────
   3 5 6 1
   1 1 1
```

Again, any total over 9 carry the tens digit to the next column.

6 Check your answer against your estimate. Does it look right? If not, go back to step 2.

3561 is very close to 3550.

Practice questions

1 Find the total of 648, 93 and 8752.

2 Increase 8654 by 7985.

3 What is 675 more than 8675 plus 938?

4 Add together 745, 8, 7385 and 68.

Subtraction

To achieve Level 4, you need to be able to subtract numbers, including some greater than 1000.

Let's practise!

1 Read the question then read it again.

'find the difference between'… It's a subtraction sum.

2 Picture the numbers. Estimate an answer.

Round the numbers and estimate:
4700 − 500 = 4200

3 Line up the digits in the correct columns.

```
Th H T U
   4 7 3 4
 −   4 9 7
 _________
```

4 Start with the right hand (units) column and subtract the bottom number from the top. If the bottom number is bigger then 'exchange' a ten from the tens.

```
Th H T U
   4 7 3²4¹
 −   4 9 7
 _________
         3 7
```

5 Repeat with the tens column, remembering to exchange if the bottom number is bigger than the top number. Repeat with the hundreds and then the thousands.

```
Th H T U
   4⁶7¹²3²4¹
 −   4 9 7
 _________
   4 2 3 7
```

6 Check your answer against your estimate. Does it look right? If not, go back to step 2.

Our estimate was 4200. Pretty close to the right answer! That's great.

Practice questions

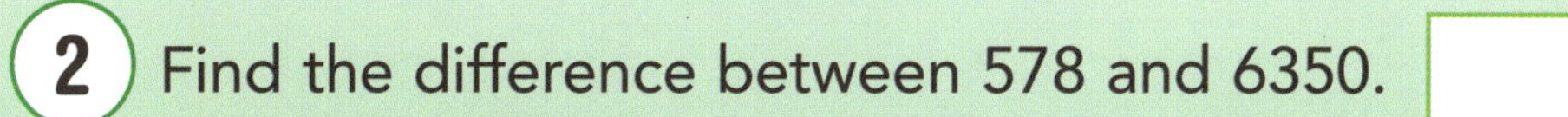

1 Subtract 6754 from 8572.

2 Find the difference between 578 and 6350.

3 What is 6492 minus 879?

4 Decrease 7563 by 777.

Adding and subtracting decimals

Achieving Level 4 means knowing how to add and subtract decimals.
When we add or subtract decimals we must line up the decimal points.

Let's practise!

1 Read the question and read it again.

2 Write the numbers. Estimate an answer.

5.76 is nearly 6 and 18.6 is nearly 19.
6 kg + 19 kg = 25 kg

3 Write the numbers, lining up the decimal points.

```
   5 . 7 6
+ 1 8 . 6
```

4 Fill in any spaces in the columns with 0 then calculate the sum.

```
  0 5 . 7 6
+ 1 8 . 6 0
  2 4 . 3 6
    1 1
```

5 Does it look right? If not, go back to step 3 and check you have lined up the decimal points.

24.36 kg is close to 25 kg.

Practice questions

Use the flow chart to work out these additions.

1 7.84 + 6.97

2 64.7 m + 58.8 m

3 £2.87 + £16.65

Find the difference between these numbers.

4 53.75 and 24.58

5 6.75 and 12.8

6 56.34 g and 28.69 g

Multiplying by 10 and 100

At Level 4 you have to multiply whole numbers by 10 and 100.

Multiplication

To multiply a whole number by 10, push the digits one place to the left and add a zero to fill the space, e.g. $68 \times 10 = 680$.

To multiply a whole number by 100, push the digits two places to the left and add two zeros, e.g. $68 \times 100 = 6800$.

Let's practise!

1	Read the question and read it again.	$346 \times 10 = ?$
2	Remember the rules!	To multiply a number by 10, we push the digits one place to the left and add a zero.
3	Calculate.	H T U Th H T U 3 4 6 × 10 becomes 3 4 6 0
4	Check your answer. If it doesn't look correct, go back to step 2.	Does 3460 look sensible? We've multiplied by 10 so we only add one zero. Our answer looks correct.

Tip ★ To multiply 30 by 40, use $3 \times 4 = 12$ and then push the digits two places to the left, so $30 \times 40 = 1200$.

Practice questions

1. $76 \times 10 = \boxed{}$
2. $580 \times \boxed{} = 58000$
3. $543 \times 100 = \boxed{}$
4. $40 \times 20 = \boxed{}$
5. $60 \times 300 = \boxed{}$
6. $\boxed{} \times 10 = 650$

Dividing by 10 and 100

At Level 4 you have to divide whole numbers by 10 and 100.

To divide a whole number by 10, push the digits one place to the right, so you lose a zero, e.g. $680 \div 10 = 68$.

To divide a whole number by 100, push the digits two places to the right, removing two zeros, e.g. $6800 \div 100 = 68$.

Let's practise!

1	Read the question and read it again.	$6500 \div$ ☐ $= 65$
2	Remember the rules!	How many places to the right have the digits been pushed?
3	Calculate.	Push the digits once: $6500 \rightarrow 650$ We need to get 65, so push the digits again. $650 \rightarrow 65$ The digits moved 2 places so the answer is 100.
4	Check the answer. If it looks sensible, write it in the box. If not, go back to step 2.	$6500 \div 100 = 65$ looks fine. Multiplying is the opposite of dividing so we can check by doing $65 \times 100 = 6500$. We are correct!

Tip ★ For $640 \div 80$ we can push the digits to the right, removing a zero, to make $64 \div 8 = 8$.

Practice questions

1 $8400 \div 10 =$ ☐   **2** $2500 \div$ ☐ $= 250$ **3** $5000 \div 100 =$ ☐

4 $75{,}000 \div$ ☐ $= 750$ **5** $4500 \div 50 =$ ☐   **6** $42{,}000 \div 600 =$ ☐

Short multiplication

At Level 4 short multiplication is two- or three-digit numbers multiplied by a single-digit number. You can use grids like the one in the flow chart for these calculations.

Let's practise!

1 Read the question then read it again.

'product of' … that's multiplication!

2 Picture the numbers. Estimate an answer.

Mmm …
500×10 …
Around 5000?

3 Partition the numbers and draw a grid.

×	400	80	2
9			

4 Multiply the numbers.

×	400	80	2
9	3600	720	18

5 Add up the answers.

$3600 + 720 + 18 = 4338$

6 Check your answers. Does it look right? If not, go back to step 2.

What did I estimate the answer was? About 5000.

7 Check your answer against your estimate. Does it look right? If not, go back to step 2.

Our answer was fairly close to the estimate. Yes! We were correct.

Practice questions

1 $486 \times 4 =$

2 $635 \times 8 =$

3 What is the product of 742 and 6?

4 Multiply 805 by 7.

5 Times 694 by 5.

6 What is 379 multiplied by 9?

Short division

At Level 4 short division is two- or three-digit numbers divided by a single-digit number. Remember, division is the inverse (or opposite) of multiplication.

Let's practise!

1	Read the question and read it again.	'divided by' … that's division.
2	Write the numbers. What is the task?	How many times does 5 fit into 366?
3	One way of dividing is to put the first number into a 'cage' and divide the other number into it.	$366 \div 5$. 366 is the first number. 5 ⟌ 3 6 6

4	Work through the division.	Think about the hundreds. There are 3 hundreds. You are trying to make groups of 5. If you only have 3 you can't make any groups of 5 so put the hundreds in with the tens to make 36 tens.
		
		5 ⟌ 3 ³6 6
		
		So how many 5s make 36? That's 7 and 1 ten left over. Put the left-over ten with the units.
		
		     7
		5 ⟌ 3 ³6 ¹6
		
		Next, how many 5s in 16? That's 3 and 1 left over.
		
		   7 3 r1
		5 ⟌ 3 ³6 ¹6
		
		Our answer is 73 r1.

5	Check your answer.	73 rounds to 70 and $5 \times 70 = 350$ Our answer is sensible!

Practice questions

1 $677 \div 2 =$ ☐

2 $532 \div 3 =$ ☐

3 $614 \div 4 =$ ☐

4 $953 \div 6 =$ ☐

Angles

To achieve Level 4 you need to understand about angles. They are measured in degrees. A right angle is 90 degrees (90°).

Practice questions

Put these angles in order of size, the smallest first.

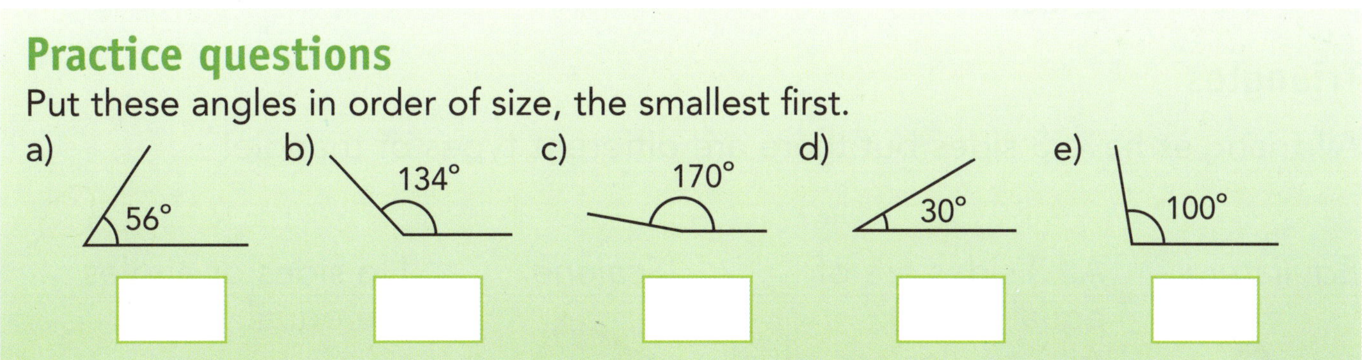

You need to measure angles with a protractor.

Let's practise!

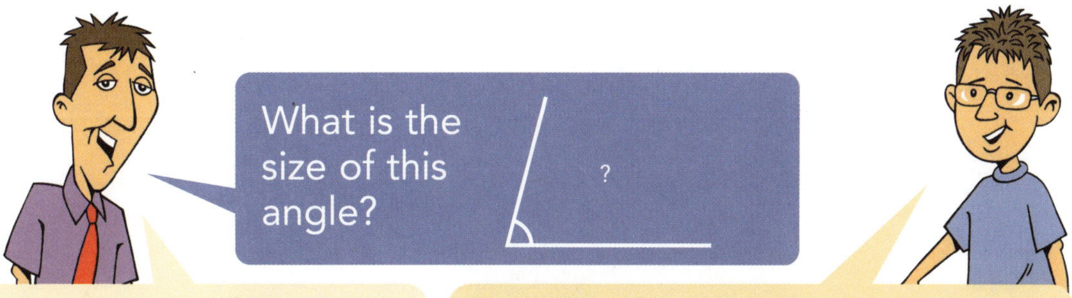

1	Read the question and read it again.	We need the size of the angle.
2	Estimate the angle.	It is less than a right angle – about 70°.
3	Decide what equipment you need.	You need a protractor to measure an angle.
4	Place the protractor on the angle.	Put the cross on the protractor over the corner of the angle. Put the zero line along one of the sides.
5	Measure the angle.	The other line is at 75 so the angle is 75°.
6	Does your answer look sensible?	Yes, it is a little less than a right angle.

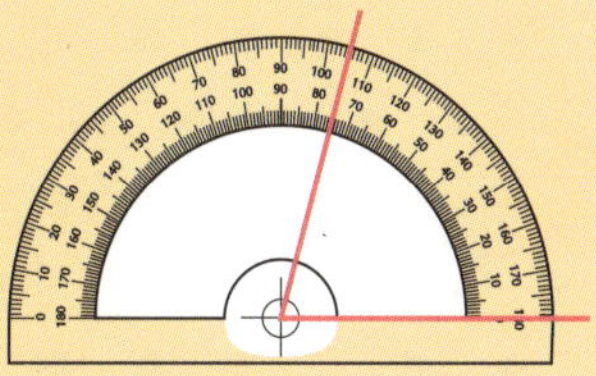

Tip	★ **Count round the scale from 0.**

Practice questions

Measure these angles accurately.

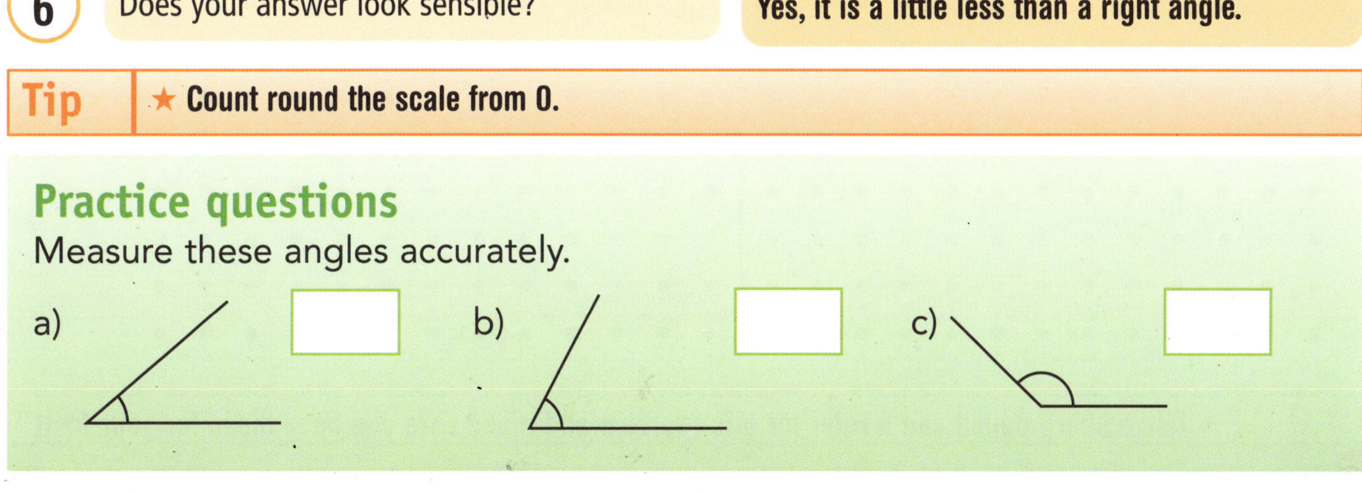

2-D shapes

To achieve Level 4 in mathematics you will need to know all about 2-D shapes, including triangles and rectangles. You will also need to know how to draw them on grids.

Triangles

All triangles have 3 sides but there are different types of triangle!

Equilateral

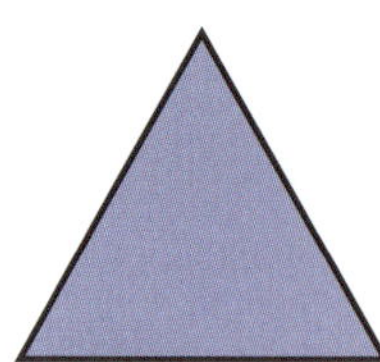

All 3 sides are of equal length.
All 3 angles are equal in size.

Scalene

No sides or angles are equal.

Isoceles

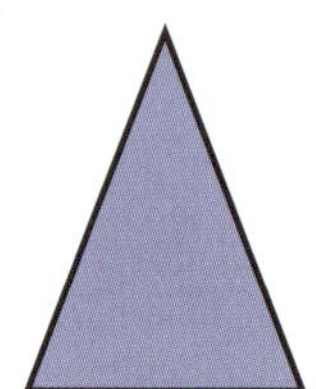

Two sides are equal.
Two angles are equal.

Right-angled triangle

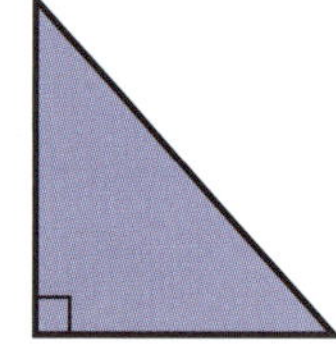

One of the angles is a right angle.

Use these grids to draw three examples of each type of triangle.
Make sure the points (or vertices) of each shape are on the dots.

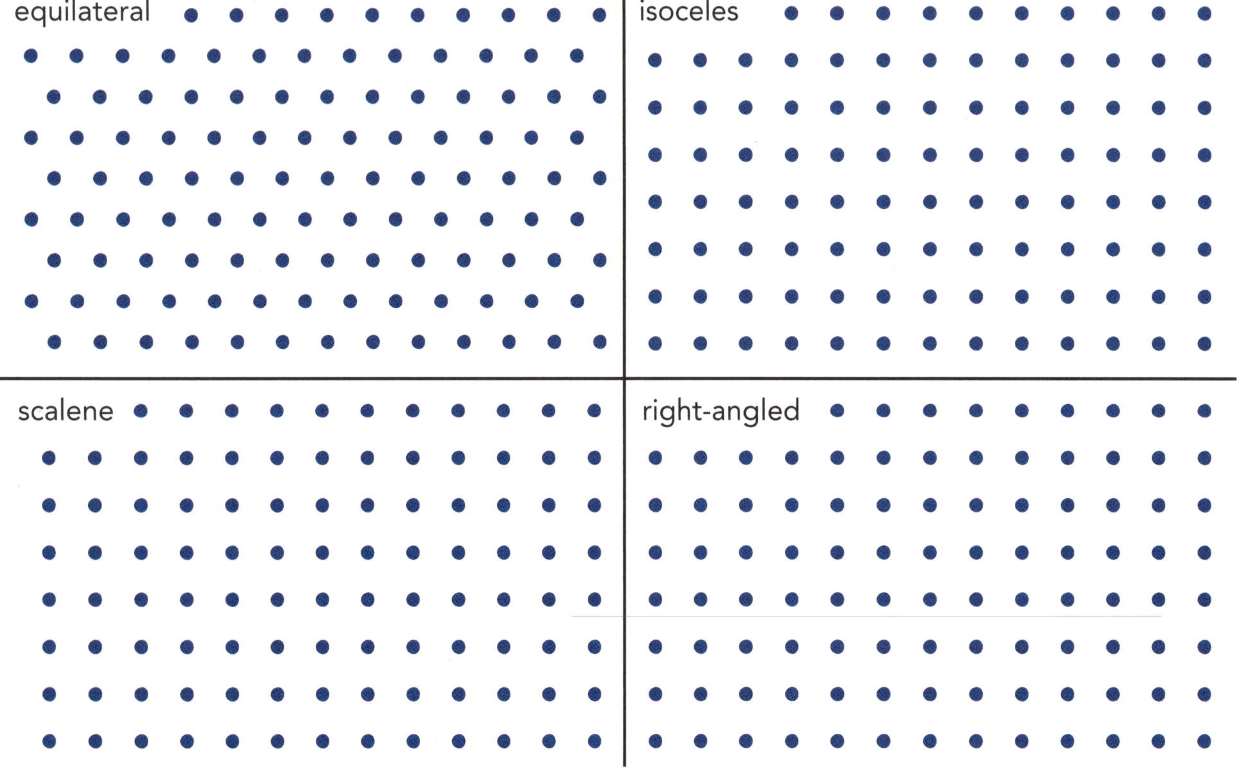

| Tip | ★ Use a sharp pencil and a ruler for this exercise and make sure you have these for your test! |

Properties of other 2-D shapes

To achieve Level 4 there are other things about 2-D shapes you need to learn.

Parallel sides

Two lines that are always the same distance apart are called parallel lines.

Think of railway lines – they **must** be parallel for a train to stay on the track.

Perpendicular lines

Two straight lines that make a right angle when they cross are called perpendicular lines.

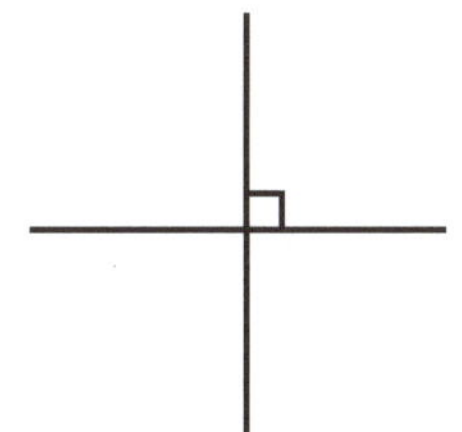

Rectangles

It is important to learn and remember these properties of a rectangle.

a) All four angles are right angles.

b) The opposite sides are parallel and equal.

c) The diagonals bisect each other (dashed blue lines on the diagram).

d) There are two lines of symmetry (dashed red lines on the diagram).

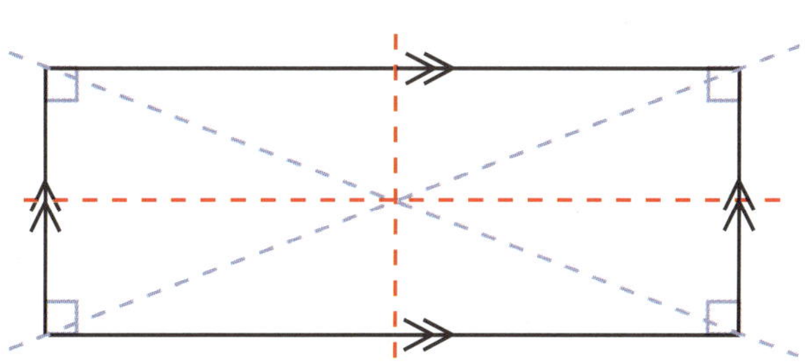

Parallel = lines that never meet and are always the same distance from one another. This symbol shows when two lines are parallel ≪ .

Bisect = when the lines cross they cut each other in half.

Square = a rectangle with four equal sides!

Practice activities

1. Draw 3 rectangles of different sizes.
   - Use a protractor to draw the angles accurately.
   - Use a ruler to draw the sides accurately.

2. For each rectangle:
   - Mark two pairs of parallel lines.
   - Label the length of each side.
   - Draw in the lines of symmetry.
   - Draw one diagonal and measure its length.

Moving 2-D shapes

Reflections of simple shapes in a mirror line

To achieve Level 4 you need to be able to reflect a shape in a mirror line placed at any angle.

Let's practise!

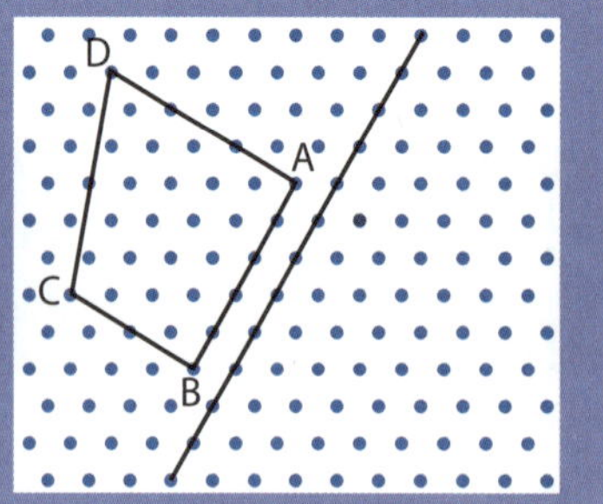

1	Read the question and read it again.	**We need to reflect the shape in the mirror line.**
2	Place a mirror on the mirror line.	**Use the mirror to see its reflection.**
3	Draw the corners of the reflected shape.	**Count the spots from point A to the mirror line and move that number of spots from the line in the opposite direction.**

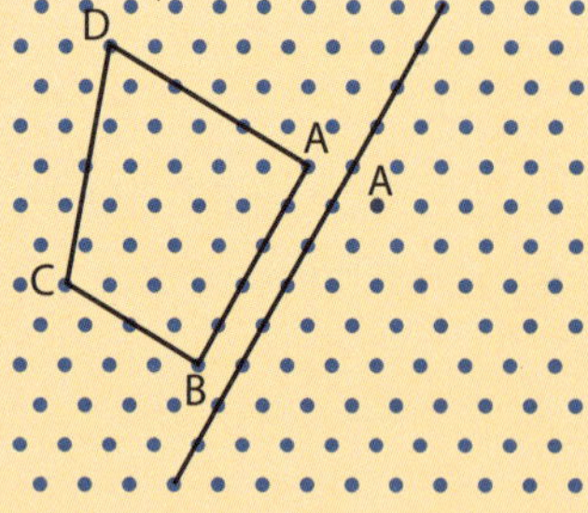

Repeat with the other corners.

4	Complete the shape.	**Use a ruler to join the points.**

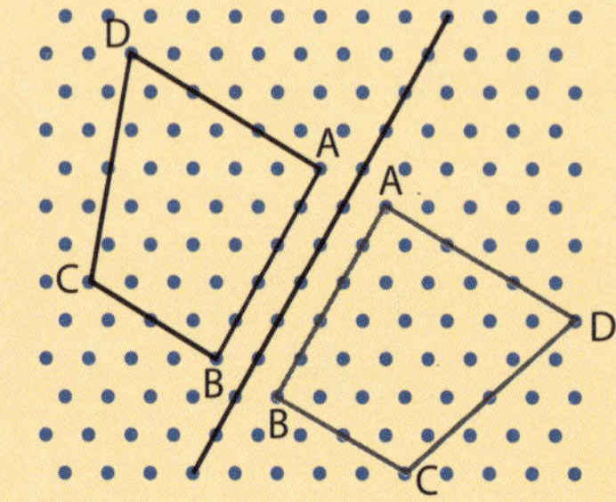

5	Check your answer.	**Make sure the shape you have drawn is in the same position as the one in the mirror and is a 'flipped over' version of the original shape.**

Practice questions

Now try these reflections in the mirror lines:

1 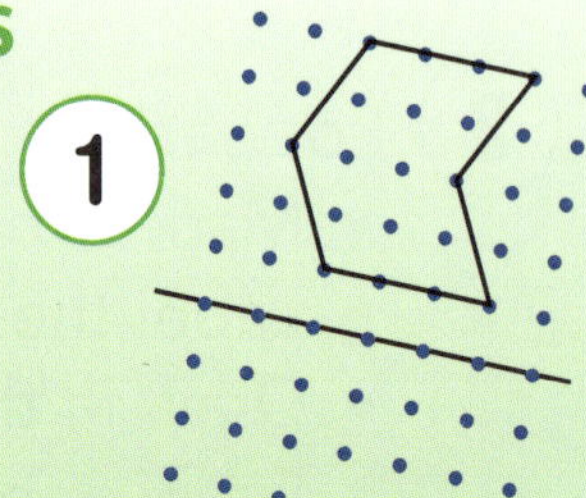

2 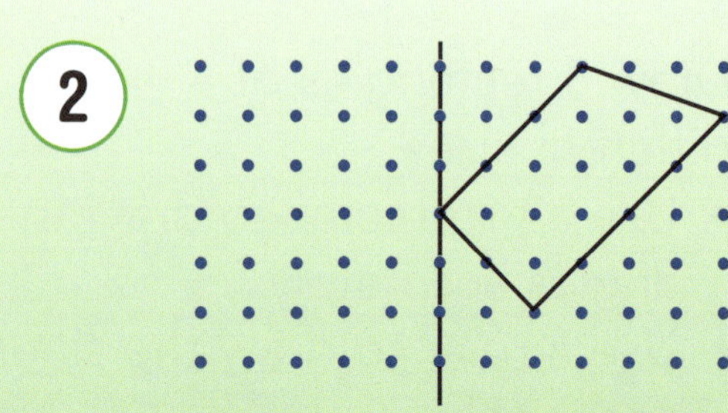

Rotational symmetry

To achieve Level 4 you also need to understand rotational symmetry. Remember, rotate just means turn. It's easy to turn a shape around!

Let's practise!

1 Read the question and read it again.

Rotate means turn – we need to see how many times we can turn the shape around and it will fit on itself.

2 Trace the shape and mark a starting point X and the centre.

3 Find the order of rotational symmetry.

Turn the tracing paper round the centre and see how many times the shape will cover itself **EXACTLY** before the X is back where it started.

4 Check your answer and write it in the answer box.

It fitted 8 times, so it has rotational symmetry of order 8.

Practice questions

Write the order of rotational symmetry of these shapes:

1 a)  b)  c) 

2 Rotate this shape clockwise once through a right angle about A.

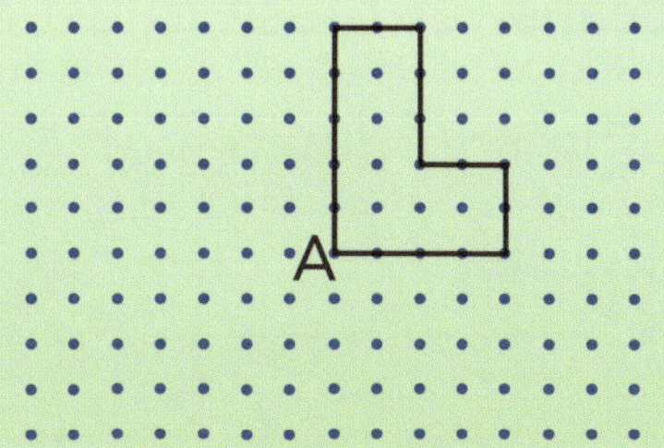

| Tip | ★ **Order of rotational symmetry** means *the number of times* you can turn a shape so it fits exactly on top of itself. |

Using coordinates

To achieve Level 4 you need to be able to read and plot coordinates as they are used on grids, like maps and charts.

On a grid the numbers going **along** are on the **x** axis. It is always horizontal. The numbers going **up** and **down** are on the **y** axis. It is always vertical.

Let's practise!

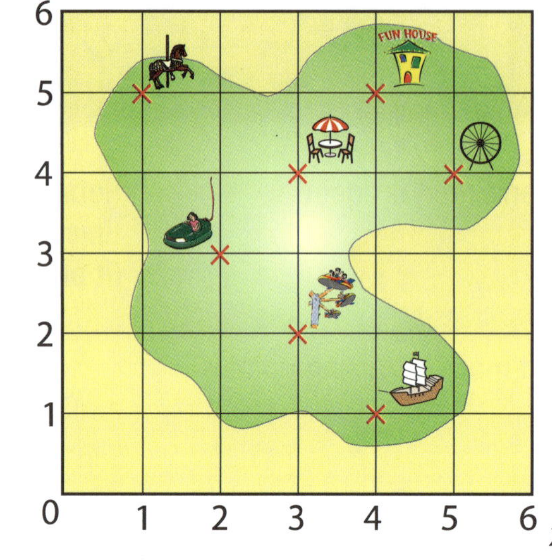

Look at this map of a theme park. What are the coordinates of the pirate ship?

1	Read the question and read it again.	We are being asked to find a coordinate pair.
2	Write the numbers.	We need to use the numbers on the map.
3	Find the place named.	The pirate ship is 4 across and 1 up. That is the coordinates (4, 1).
4	Check your answer.	If we find (4, 1) on the map, that is where the pirate ship is.

Practice questions

Use the map to answer these questions.

1) What are the coordinates of:

   a) the flying cars? ☐   b) the café? ☐   c) the carousel? ☐

2) Which ride is at these points?

   a) (2, 3) _______________   b) (4, 5) _______________

Coordinate problems often use shapes

Let's practise!

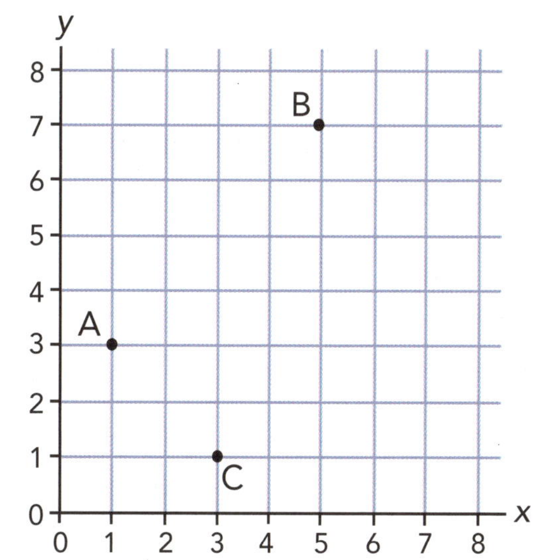

1 Read the question and read it again.	**We have to make a rectangle.**
2 Study the points given.	**There are three points.**
3 Look for clues from the shape and the points.	**A rectangle has right angles. Joining A to B and then A to C makes a right angle.** 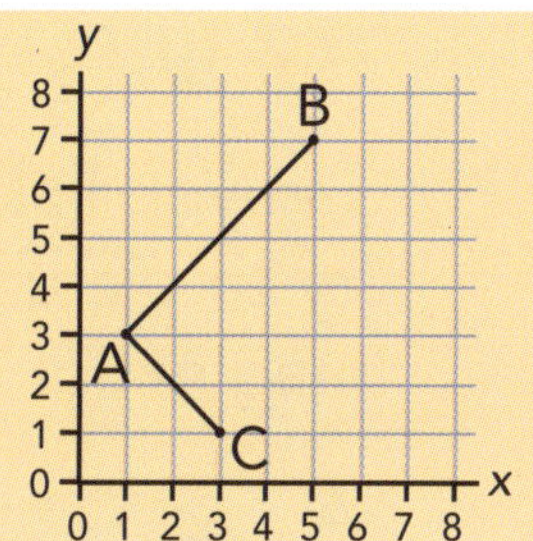
4 Complete the shape.	**Make right angles at points B and C and draw the lines. Look for where the lines cross.** 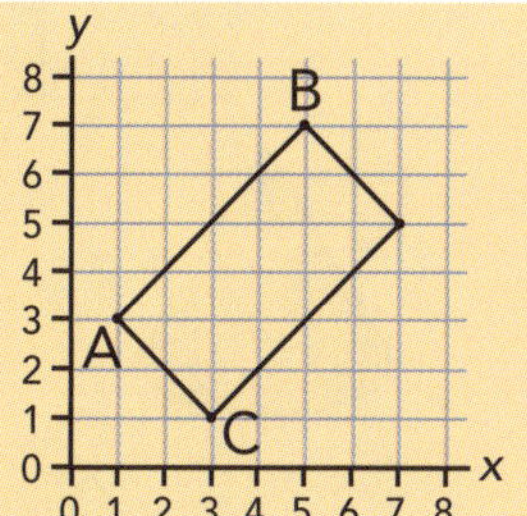
5 Check where the new point is.	**The lines cross at (7, 5) so that is the fourth point.**

Practice question

Write the coordinates of a fourth point that makes a square.

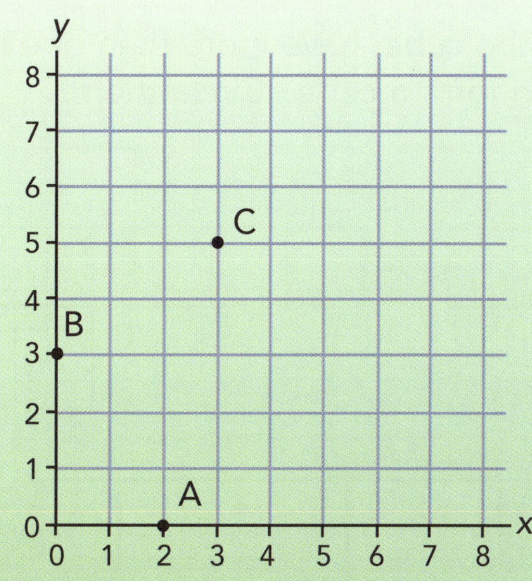

3-D shapes

To get a Level 4 in mathematics you have to be able to imagine what a 3-D shape would look like if it was 'unfolded' – that is, when it is a 'net'.

The net of a solid shape is what it looks like when it has been opened out and laid flat.

Imagine unfolding a box of coloured pencils so that the box is just one piece of card.

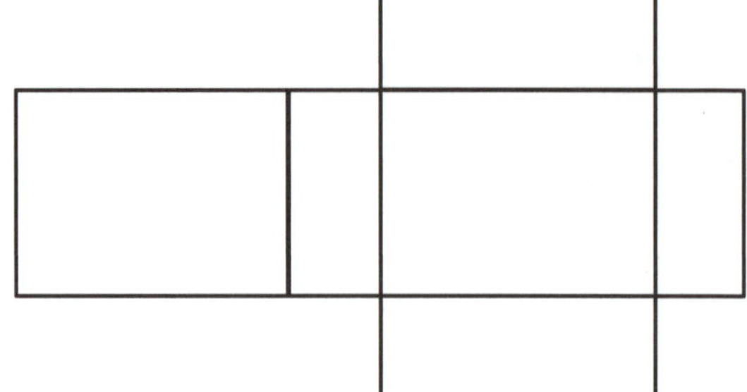

Practice questions

1) Can you link the nets to the 3-D shapes? Draw a line to match them up. Try to picture the nets folding themselves up in front of your eyes. Imagination is important in maths you know!

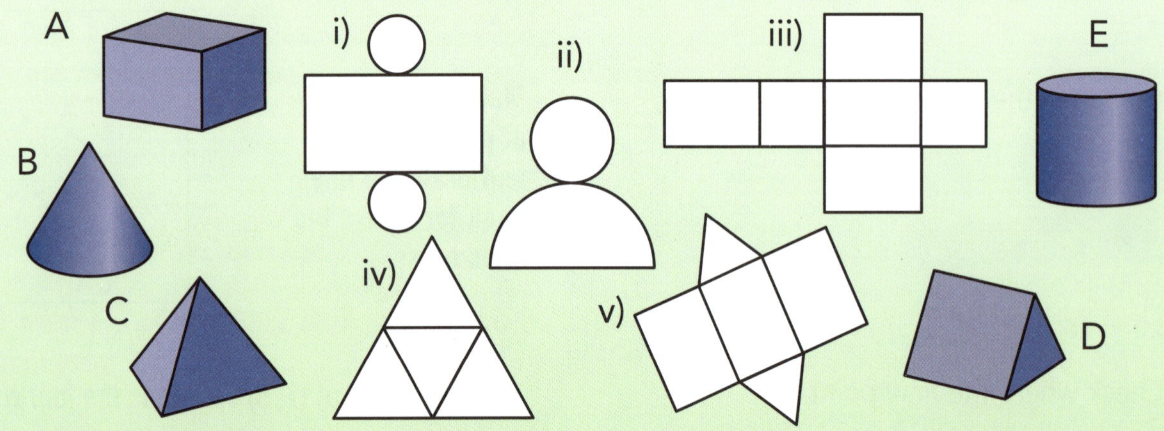

2) Some shapes, like the cube, have more than one net. Can you see which of these nets would form a cube? Circle them.

Completing a 3-D shape

A popular question is to ask you to visualise 3-D shapes that have blocks missing.

Let's practise!

1	Read the question then read it again.	**What are you being asked to do?**
2	Picture the complete shape in your head.	**What would it look like? Think about each block. Don't forget to include the blocks you can't see.**
3	Work out the dimensions of the shape.	**'Dimensions' means how many blocks long, wide and high it is. This shape is 4 blocks long, 4 wide and 3 high.**
4	Calculate the total number of blocks if the shape was complete.	**Right, that's $4 \times 4 \times 3 = 48$. 48 blocks would make up the entire cuboid.**
5	Calculate how many blocks are in each layer.	**There should be 3 layers of 16 blocks because $3 \times 16 = 48$. Cool!**
6	Count how many blocks are missing from each layer to get your answer.	**Bottom layer: 3 missing. Middle layer: 5 missing. Top layer: 9 missing. $3 + 5 + 9 = 17$ blocks missing.**
7	Does your answer look right? If not, go back to step 1.	**Yes, it does. We need 17 blocks to turn the shape into a cuboid.**

Practice questions

How many blocks would it take to complete these cuboids?

Measures

To achieve Level 4 in mathematics it is important that you know the following things about measures.

- Which units of measure to use when measuring length, mass and capacity.

- Which instruments to use when measuring length, mass and capacity.

- How to read those instruments.

Use the table on this page to learn about the first two!

	Length			Mass (weight)			Capacity		
	Unit	Instrument	Example	Unit	Instrument	Example	Unit	Instrument	Example
Small size	mm	Ruler	Raisin Sunflower seed	g	Scales	Newspaper Chocolate bar	ml	Teaspoon	Bottle of food colouring for cakes
Medium size	cm	Ruler Metre rule	DVD case Your foot	kg	Bathroom scales	A bag of cement Yourself	cl	Measuring jug	Can of cola Glass of milk
Large size	m km	Tape measure Metre wheel Tachometer	Distance you can ride a bike	kg tonne	Large scales Weigh bridge	Rhinoceros Tractor	l	Container of known capacity	Capacity of aquarium Swimming pool

Here are some questions about the table.

1. Name something you would measure in centimetres. ________________________

2. Name something you would measure in centilitres. ________________________

3. What instrument would you use to measure the weight of the newspaper?

____

4. What instrument would you use to measure the length of a sunflower seed? ________________________

5. Think of two things not in the table you could measure in:

    a) kg ________________ and ________________

    b) l ________________ and ________________

    c) km ________________ and ________________

Reading scales

At Level 4 it is important that you understand how to read instruments of measure, most of which use scales. The scale can go up in different amounts on different measuring instruments.

Let's practise!

1 Read the question and read it again.

We are dealing with measures so we need to be accurate.

2 Think about the numbers.

The numbers go up in 100s.

3 Check the unit on the scale.

The scales are marked in grams (g).

4 If the measure is on a numbered level, read off that level.

It is between 200 g and 300 g.

5 If the measure is between numbers, work out what each mark is worth and count forwards or backwards.

Each 100 g is split into 4 sections.
100 g ÷ 4 = 25 g so each section is 25 g.
200 g + 1 mark = 200 g + 25 g = 225 g.

6 Is your answer sensible?

The point is just past 200 g so 225 g is sensible.

Practice question
What is the length of the car?

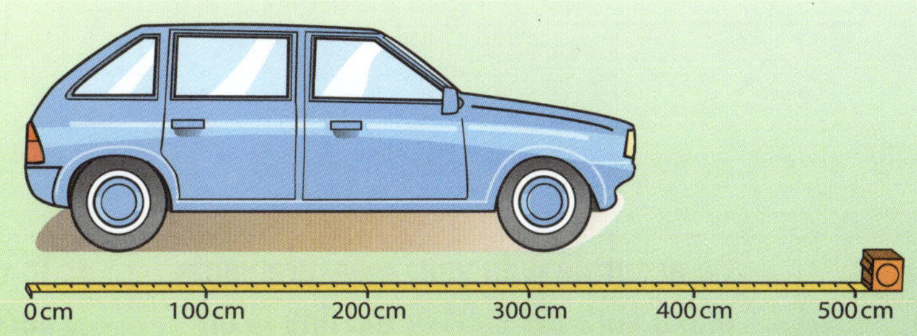

Perimeters of simple shapes

To achieve Level 4 you need to know how to work out the perimeter of a shape. The perimeter of a shape is the distance all the way around its edge.

Let's practise!

1	Read the question and read it again.	'Perimeter of'. We are being asked to measure the distance around the shape.
2	First, work out the length of the sides.	This is the important part! Measure accurately and write on the sides as you work them out. The longer sides are 6.2 cm and the shorter sides are 2.8 cm.
3	Add up all the lengths.	6.2 cm + 6.2 cm + 2.8 cm + 2.8 cm = 18 cm
4	Does your answer look sensible?	The perimeter of the shape is 18 cm.

Practice questions

Find the perimeter of these shapes.

a) 

b) 

Tips	★ Be accurate with your measurements. Make sure the start of the line is on the zero on your ruler.	★ To remember what perimeter means think of a perimeter fence, which goes ALL THE WAY ROUND a building like a prison or a military base.

Areas of shapes by counting

To achieve Level 4 you will need to find the area of a tricky shape that has been drawn onto squared paper.

> The area of a shape is the amount of the surface it covers.
>
> Make sure the units you write are always squared, e.g. cm^2 or m^2.

Let's practise!

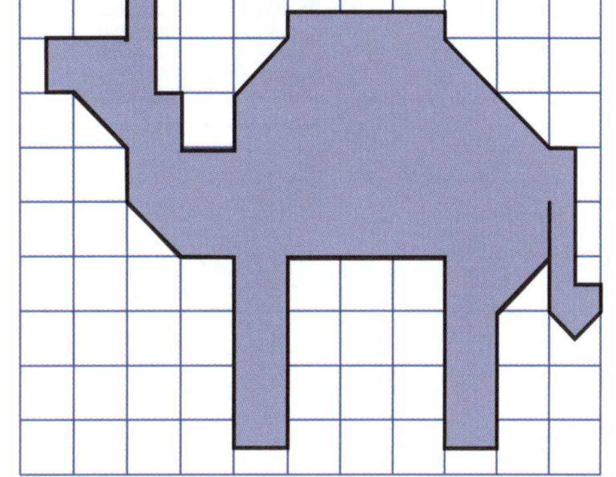

1	Read the question then read it again.	It is the shaded squares we have to count.
2	Start by counting the whole squares, ticking them off as each is counted.	Start at the top row and move your finger along to the end counting any whole squares. Repeat on the next row. Jot down the total: 31 squares.
3	Now count the $\frac{3}{4}$ shaded squares.	OK, start from the top row and work downwards. Jot down the total: one $\frac{3}{4}$ square.
4	Now count the $\frac{1}{2}$ shaded squares.	There are sixteen $\frac{1}{2}$ squares.
5	Now count the $\frac{1}{4}$ shaded squares.	Back to the top again. Work carefully – there is one $\frac{1}{4}$ square.
6	Now add together all the fractions.	One times $\frac{3}{4} = \frac{3}{4}$; sixteen halves = 8; one quarter $= \frac{1}{4}$. That makes 9 whole squares.
7	Add the units and square your answer. Does it look sensible? If not, go back to step 2.	31 whole squares + 9 whole squares = 40 cm^2. This looks sensible.

Grouping data

To achieve Level 4 you need to know about grouped data graphs.

Here is a chart showing the number of questions answered correctly by 16 children in a school quiz with 30 questions. We wanted to find out how many children scored between 16 and 20 marks.

This looks quite complicated! We can make it easier if we group the scores and then compare them.

Look at the new chart and answer the questions below.

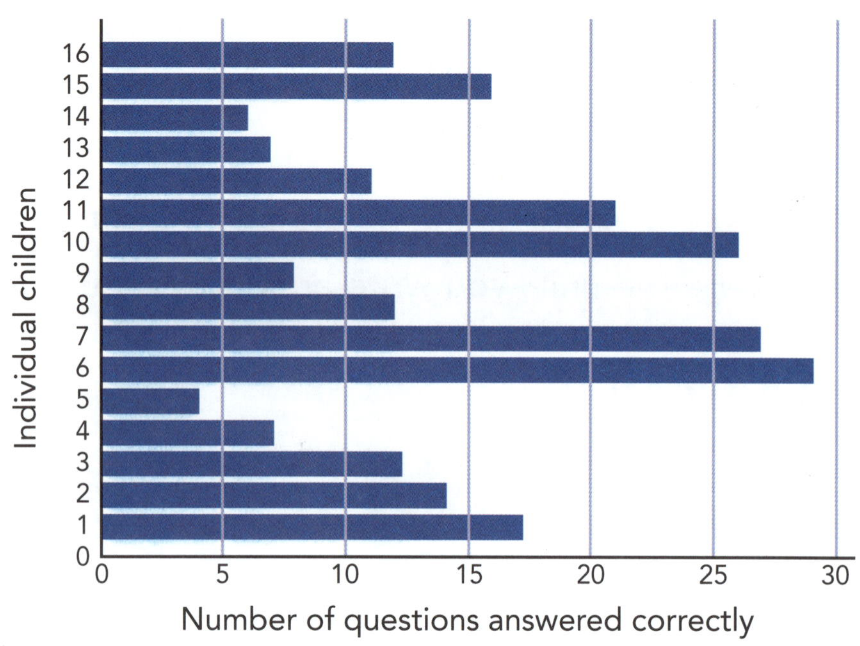

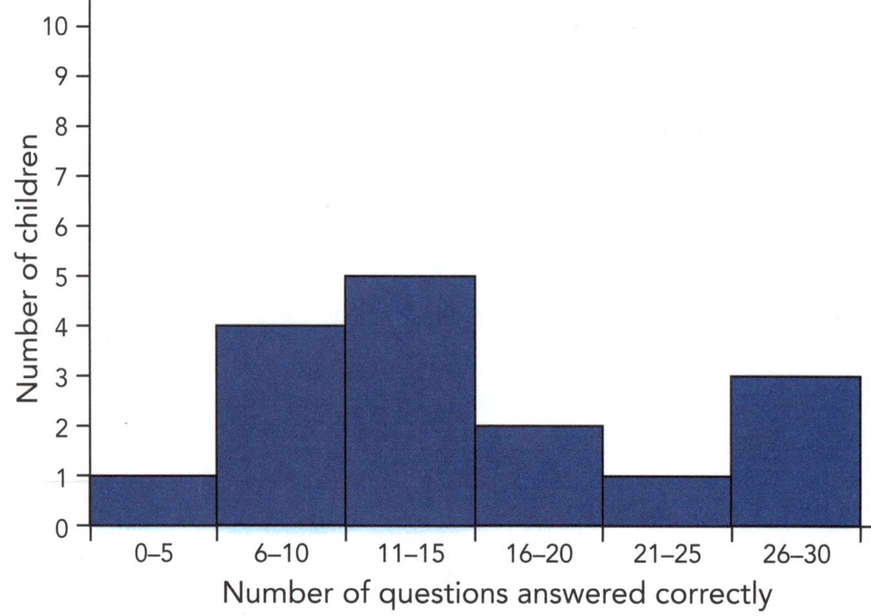

Questions

1. How many children scored between 16 and 20 marks?

2. How many children scored more than 15 marks?

3. What was the second most common range of scores in the quiz?

4. How many children scored fewer than 21 marks?

5. Look at both of the charts. Did anyone get all the questions right?

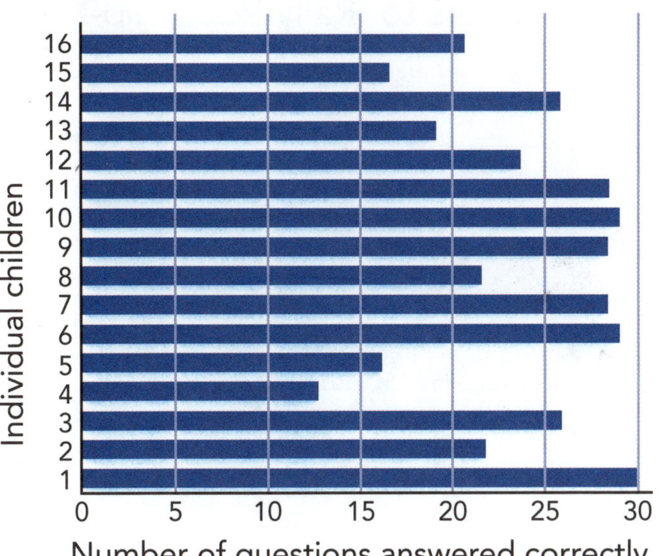

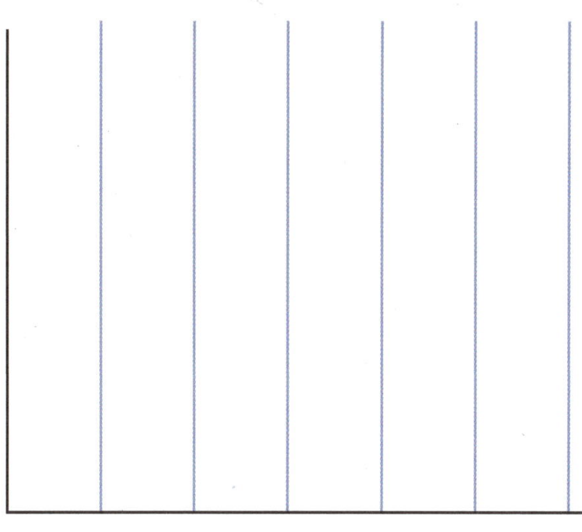

(1) Read the question then read it again.

(2) Group the data in equal amounts. Mark on your axis.

(3) Tally the number for each group of data.

OK. The first group is 0–5. How many children scored 0–5? None. Now the next group. None again. Now the 11–15 group. Ah! 1. Next the 16–20 group ... 3. Next the 21–25 group ... 4. Finally the 26–30 group ... 8.

(4) Draw in the bars.

The most common score is now between 26 and 30.

(5) Check your results. Do they look sensible?

Yes, the children scored much higher. This looks right.

Tips ★ Think clearly. Work step by step. ★ When handling data, a rough piece of paper can be useful to make notes or tally information.

Line graphs

Line graphs are an important part of Level 4. A graph with **time** on the **x** axis (horizontal) and **numbers** on the **y** axis (vertical) often shows a set of points joined by a line. Only the points have a value – the line between just shows the trend.

Here is a line graph showing the number of visitors to 'Rally Road' go-kart arena over the course of a year.

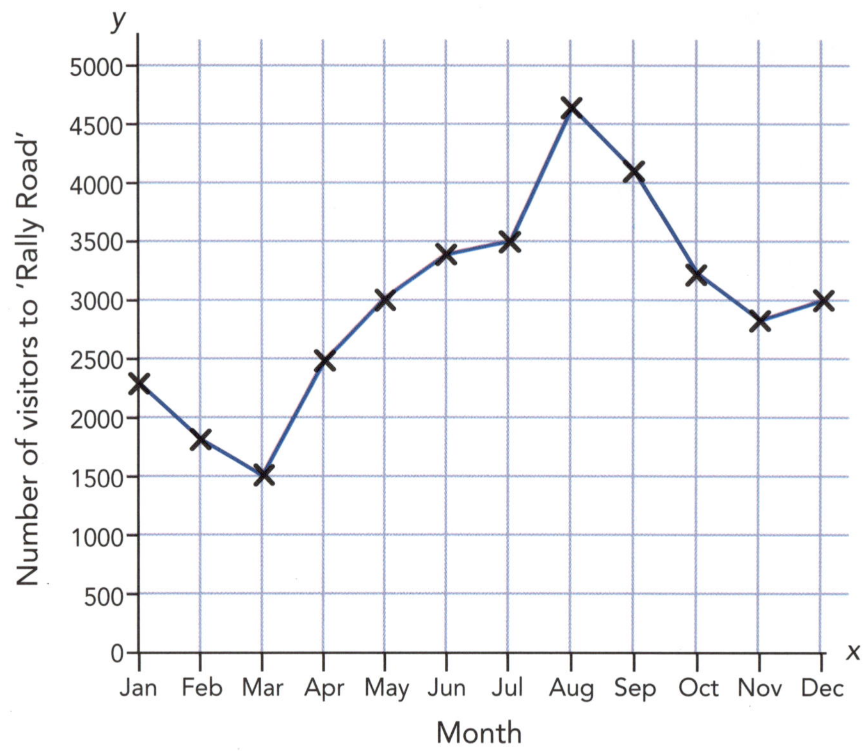

Try answering these questions:

1. a) Which was the least popular month? __________

   b) How many visitors did Rally Road have in that month? __________

2. The number of visitors first fell between __________ and __________.

3. In which month were there 2800 visitors? __________

4. Why do you think there were most visitors in August?

   ____

5. How many visitors do you think there were in June? __________

> **Tip** ★ **When reading graphs, make sure you follow the lines carefully across and up and down. Using a ruler can help.**

Let's practise!

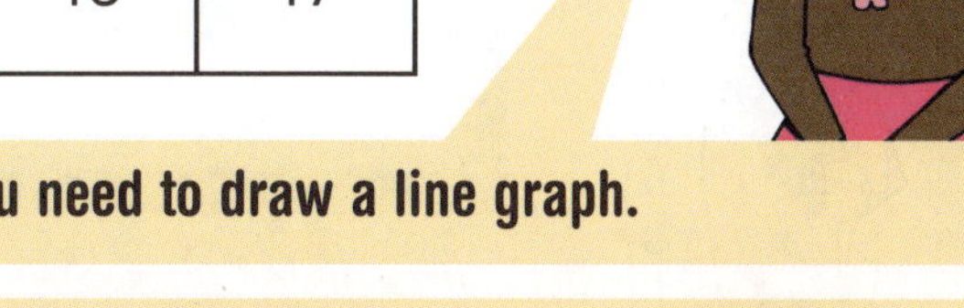

Day	Mon	Tues	Wed	Thurs	Fri	Sat	Sun
Number of goals	3	5	9	14	9	13	17

(1) Read the question then read it again.

You need to draw a line graph.

(2) Decide which information fits on each axis.

The days (time) should go on the x axis and the goals scored (number) should go on the y axis.

(3) Decide on a scale.

We need a scale for the number of goals. The highest number is 17 and our grid is 12 squares high – we need to go up in steps of 2.

(4) Plot the points.

This must be accurate. Start at Monday on the x axis and work along to Sunday.

(5) Join the points to show the trend.

Does it match the results table?

Put the information on the graph using the flow chart to help you.

Then answer the questions below.

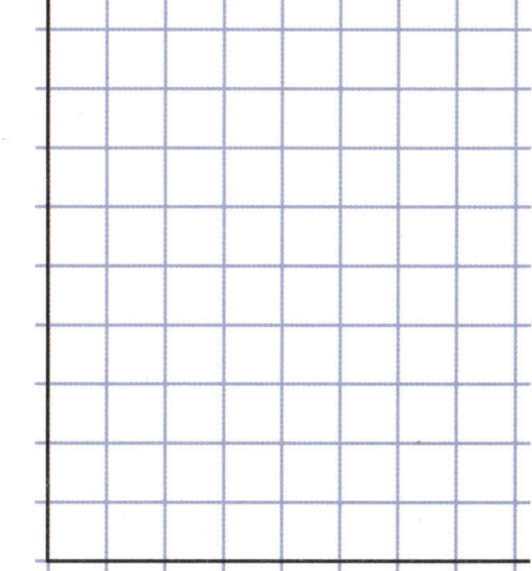

(1) How many days did Buxworth School score more than 8 goals?

____

(2) Between which two days did their score improve the most?

_______________ and ______________

(3) a) What was the general trend over the week for the number of goals scored?

____

b) Which day was different to the general trend? _______________.

Tip | ★ **Always use a sharp pencil when plotting points – it helps you to be more accurate.**

Finding the range

To achieve Level 4 you will need to find the range of a series of data.

Let's practise!

1 Read the question then read it again.	
2 Think about the question.	The range is the difference between the lowest and highest value.
3 Picture the numbers.	Put them in order, lowest first: £8.99, £10, £10.98 and £14.49
4 Study the numbers.	The most expensive is £14.49. The cheapest is £8.99. What is the difference between these costs?
5 Calculate your answer.	£14.49 – £8.99 = £5.50
6 If your answer looks sensible, write it in the box. If not, go back to step 3 and try again.	

Practice question

Talib compares the number of kilometres driven by six teachers last year.

Mr Hartley 8637 km, Mrs Cooper 9642 km, Mrs Butcher 3972 km
Ms Wright 6539 km, Mrs Mellor 9853 km, Mr Chan 5740 km

What was the range of kilometres driven?

Tips	★ Scan the list and mark the lowest number.	★ Check through the list to see if it really is the lowest. Repeat for the highest number.

Finding the mode

To achieve Level 4 you need to understand the mode.

Let's practise!

1 Read the question then read it again.

2 Think about the question.

The mode is another name for the most common value.

3 Picture the numbers.

Make sets of the same number.

18	22	23	29
18	22	23	29
	22	23	
	22		

4 Double-check.

Make sure you haven't missed any numbers.

5 Decide on your answer.

22 occurs most often.
22 is the mode.

6 If your answer looks sensible, write it in the box. If not, go back to step 3 and try again.

Practice question

Ben counts how many people log on to his website every day for two weeks.

20 13 32 20 35 20 25 13 30 62 13 24 13 23

What is the mode for the number of hits?

Tips	★ Remember: • Mode is the most common value, • Modal means mode.	★ Always write out the numbers again and sort them. Tick off each number so you know you haven't missed any of them. This is IMPORTANT!

Number patterns

Number patterns or sequences are lists of numbers that follow a pattern. To achieve Level 4 you need to work out a sequence by finding the difference between the numbers.

Let's practise!

1. Read the question then read it again.

   There are two parts to this question. Don't forget the second part.

2. Picture the numbers.

   Starting at 27 and going upwards towards 79.

3. Look at the difference between the first two numbers that are next to each other.

   27 and 40. The difference is 13.

4. Use the difference you have found and 'test it' on the sequence.

   40 + 13 = 53
   53 + 13 = 66
   66 + 13 = 79 It fits!

5. If it fits the sequence, fill in your answer and explain the rule.

   Fill in the boxes correctly.

   | 53 | 66 |

   Explain the rule: 'Add 13 each time.'

Practice questions

Try to fill in the gaps to complete these sequences. Explain the rule you find.

1. 8, 14, ☐, 26, ☐ _______________________

2. 9, ☐, ☐, 0, –3 _______________________

3. ☐, 78, 99, ☐, ☐ _______________________

Using simple formulae

A formula is a way of explaining a rule. To achieve Level 4 you need to be able to explain a given rule in writing.

Let's practise!

1 Read the question then read it again.

It is all words. You have to work out any numbers involved.

2 Picture the numbers and the words.

The key word here is 'explain'. You also need to show that there are 12 months in a year.

3 Talk through the rule in your head.

To find the number of months in any number of years, you must multiply the number of years by 12 …

4 Test your rule. Does it work? If not, go back to step 1.

Make your test simple to avoid mistakes, e.g. 4 years = $4 \times 12 = 48$ months

5 Write your rule as simply as possible.

'The number of months in any number of years = the number of years multiplied by 12.'

6 Check your answer. Does it make sense?

Read it through to yourself. Does your formula work?

Tips

★ Rehearse your sentences in your head before you write them. When you have written them, read them back to yourself. Have you thought clearly? Have you said what you wanted to say?

★ The '=' sign means 'the same as' e.g. $2 + 2 = 4$; $2 + 2$ is the same as 4
$10 - 5 = 8 - 3$; $10 - 5$ is the same as $8 - 3$

Using and applying mathematics

To achieve Level 4 you need to be able to solve all kinds of maths problems.

The reason for learning all the different mathematical skills (multiplying, dividing, measuring, estimating and so on) is so you can use them to solve mathematical problems.

Imagine learning all the shots in tennis, like the serve, the volley, the backhand and forehand, but never actually getting to play a game! Only by using your shots in a match will you learn to be a tennis player. Likewise, only by using your mathematical skills will you learn to be a mathematician!

The flow chart opposite is designed to guide you when tackling a maths problem. It will help organise your thinking, but it won't tell you the answer – that's for you to work out for yourself.

The next few pages contain problems for you to solve. Work through the examples first and then have a go at the practice questions using the flow chart approach.

Good luck!

Problem solving

Number

These questions are all about your number skills. You must use them in the right way though!

Shape and space

These questions all require you to use your knowledge about shapes, both 2-D and 3-D.

Measures

These questions are all about real situations: going on a journey, the amount of milk a family drinks in a week and so on.

Handling data

These questions often ask you to find out information from a table or chart. They will also ask you to explain how you found out the answer!

The problem-solving flow chart

1   Read the question then read it again.

Read the question twice carefully. Let the words and numbers 'sink in'.

2   Write the numbers and highlight any key words.

Write down any numbers and key words. It might help to draw a picture or diagram.

3   Can you estimate an answer?

This depends on the question. Try to estimate using the numbers and words you jotted down in step 2.

4   Which calculations do you need to do?

Work out if you need to use +, −, × or ÷. Check if you need to do more than one calculation.

5   Work out the problem.

Do any calculations needed. Make sure you are answering the problem.

6   Is your answer sensible?

Read the question again and check that your answer is realistic. If not, go back to step 2.

Tips
- ★ Remember your 'checking the answer' skills.
- ★ Think clearly and write clearly.
- ★ Present your work so it shows what you have done.
- ★ Work step by step.
- ★ Make a problem easier (e.g. Find 24 lots of 6. Try finding 4 lots first then 20 lots.)
- ★ Take a reasonable guess at what you think might happen.
- ★ Think HOW you are working. Change your method if something isn't working.
- ★ Look for patterns in your maths.

Solving number problems

Achieved? 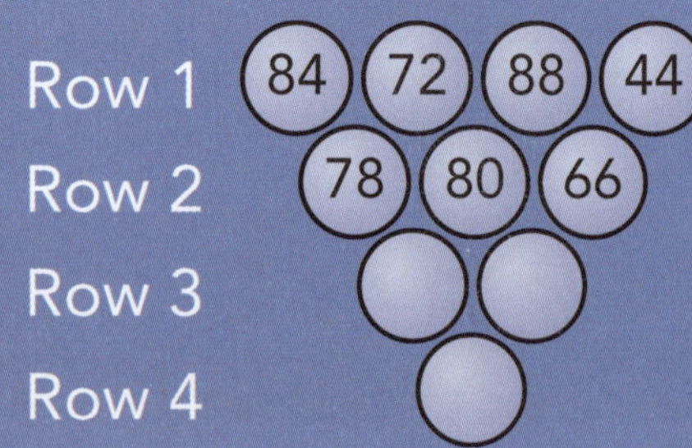

To achieve Level 4 you have to solve number problems that need more than one calculation.

The numbers in row 2 of this triangle of snooker balls have been found from the two numbers directly above them using a rule. Fill in the missing numbers and write the rule.

Rule:

1	Read the question then read it again.	**There are two things to do in this question – 'find the missing numbers' and 'write the rule'.**
2	Write the numbers and highlight any key words.	**'numbers in row 2', 'found from the two numbers directly above'. How do 84 and 72 make 78?**
3	Can you estimate an answer?	**No, because the answer is not obvious.**
4	Which calculations do you need to do?	**Work step by step. What do we have to do to get 78? Perhaps 84 + 72 or 84 – 72?**
5	Work out the problem.	**84 + 72 = 156 and 84 – 72 = 12** **Look at our answers. Can we see any link with 78? Yes! 78 is half of 156.** **The answer is 'add the two numbers and divide the answer by 2'.** **Now we can fill in the other missing numbers. (78 + 80) ÷ 2=79; (80 + 66) ÷ 2 = 73; (79 + 73) ÷ 2 = 76**
6	Is your answer sensible?	**Yes. We applied our rule and it worked!**

Solving measures problems

Achieved?

To achieve Level 4 you need to use your knowledge of measures when solving problems.

Here is a list of ingredients for banana mousse.

It feeds 4 people.

1.2 kg of bananas   6 eggs

300 ml milk   4 tablespoons caster sugar

Gordon wants to prepare banana mousse for 6 people. Can you change the amount of each ingredient so he makes enough mousse? Show your method:

1 — Read the question then read it again.

Change the amounts of the four ingredients.

2 — Write the numbers and highlight any key words.

4 people to 6. Ah! That's an increase of half as much again or 50%.

3 — Can you estimate an answer?

We can easily work out that we need $6 + (\frac{1}{2}$ of $6) = 9$ eggs and $4 + 2 = 6$ tablespoons of castor sugar. We can estimate an answer of 1.7 kg of bananas and 500 ml of milk.

4 — Which calculations do you need to do?

**(50% of 1.2 kg) + 1.2 kg
(50% of 300 ml) + 300 ml**

5 — Work out the problem.

**50% of 1.2 kg = 600 g
1200 g + 600 g = 1800 g or 1.8 kg
50% of 300 ml = 150 ml
300 ml + 150 ml = 450 ml**

6 — Is your answer sensible?

Gordon would need 1.8 kg of bananas, 450 ml of milk, 9 eggs and 6 tablespoons of sugar. Those look like sensible amounts for mousse for 6 people!

Solving shape problems

To achieve Level 4 you need to use your knowledge about shape when solving problems.

How many rectangles can you see in this shape?

Show your method:

1 Read the question then read it again.

2 Write the numbers and highlight any key words.

'How many'? We are going to need the total number of rectangles. Think how you could work in a logical step-by-step way.

3 Can you estimate an answer?

We can see 9 inside the big one straight away. That's 10. Let's double that. 20? We can only guess.

4 Which calculations do you need to do?

Work in a logical way.
How many 1 unit rectangles are there?
How many 2 unit rectangles are there?
And so on. It might help to use a table.

5 Work out the problem.

Number of units	1	2	3	4	5	6	7	8	9	Total
Number of rectangles	9	12	6	4	0	4	0	0	1	36

There are 36 rectangles in this shape.

6 Is your answer sensible?

It looks sensible because we worked it out in a step-by-step way.

Solving data handling problems

To achieve Level 4 you need to read information carefully and accurately when solving problems.

Example:

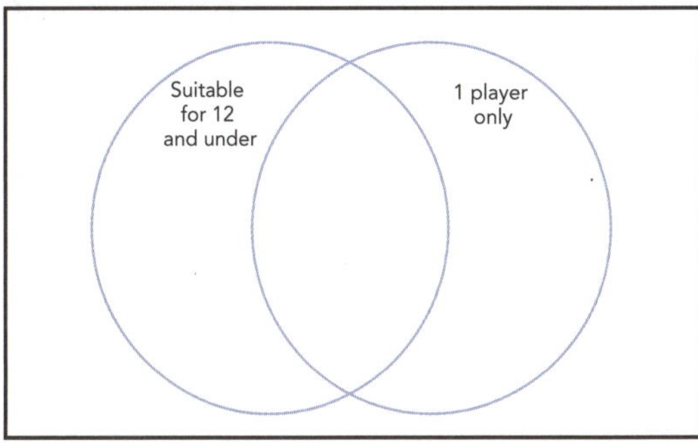

	Suitable for ages 12 and under	Not suitable for ages 12 and under
1 player only	Gran Theft Skateboard Speed Racer 2	Zombie Hunter Horror-shocker
2 or more players	Wrestling Fest	Car-jacker HALO 5

1 Read the question then read it again.

There are two different diagrams to look at and understand.

2 Write the numbers and highlight any key words.

We need to transfer information from one diagram to another. Understanding the Carroll diagram is important, e.g. *Car-jacker* and *HALO 5* are for 2 or more players and are not suitable for ages 12 and under.

3 Can you estimate an answer?

No, it would be a wild guess.

4 Which calculations do you need to do?

No calculations here. We need to put three games in the correct place on the Venn diagram.

5 What is the answer to the problem?

Wrestling Fest is for ages 12 and under but needs 2 or more players, so it goes in the left-hand circle. *Gran Theft Skateboard* is for 12 and under AND 1 player only, so it goes where the two circles meet. *HALO 5* doesn't fit in either category so goes outside both circles. Now we can write them in the correct place on the Venn diagram.

6 Is your answer sensible?

After double-checking where we have written each game, it is a sensible answer.

Key facts

Counting and understanding number

Place value
- Each number is made up of digits. The position of the digit in a number gives it its value.

Hundreds	Tens	Units	tenths	hundredths
7	8	4	3	5

$= 700 + 80 + 4 + \frac{3}{10} + \frac{5}{100} = 784.35$

Negative numbers
- Integers are just whole numbers.
- When counting from negative up to positive or from positive down to negative, **remember to count 0!**
- When counting on a number line, count to the right when adding and to the left when subtracting.

Fractions
- A fraction is part of a whole number.

$\frac{1}{2}$ the numerator / the denominator

The numerator tells you how many equal parts are used.
The denominator tells you how many equal parts there are.

Reducing a fraction to its simplest form
- To reduce a fraction to its simplest form, find a common factor which you can divide into the numerator and the denominator. For example,

$$\frac{3}{9} \div \frac{3}{3} = \frac{1}{3}$$

Fraction, decimal and percentage equivalents
- Remember as many of these as you can.

Fraction	$\frac{1}{2}$	$\frac{1}{10}$	$\frac{1}{4}$	$\frac{3}{4}$	Nearly $\frac{1}{3}$
Decimal	0.5	0.1	0.25	0.75	0.33
Percentage	50%	10%	25%	75%	33%

The vocabulary of ratio and proportion
- Ratio is 'to every'. For example, 2○ to every 3□ is ○○□□□
- Proportion is 'in every'. For example, 2○ in every 3 shapes could be shown as ○○□
- Reduce ratios and proportions to their lowest form. For example, 4:6 = 2:3.

Knowing and using number facts
- **Tables:** it is essential that you know these really well.
- **Squares:** numbers made when another number is multiplied by itself.
- **Multiples:** numbers that have been multiplied by a given number.
- **Factors:** numbers that can divide into a given number without leaving a remainder.

Checking your answers
- Inverse means opposite!
- Check addition by subtraction – and vice versa.
- Check division by multiplication – and vice versa.
- Use 'friendly numbers' when estimating: 2, 5, 10, etc.

Calculating
- Multiplying numbers by 10 and 100: Push the digits to the left once for × 10 and twice for ÷ 100.
- Dividing numbers by 10 and 100: Push the digits to the right once for ÷ 10 and twice for ÷ 100.
- Addition and subtraction of decimals:
  1. Line up the decimal points when you write out the sum.
  2. Fill empty places with a 0.
  3. Remember to put the decimal point in your answer!

Choosing your method
- Remember to look at the numbers you are working with. You might be able to use a good mental strategy rather than a written method, or it might be best to use a calculator.

Understanding shape

3-D shapes
- Vertices are corners
- Faces are flat surfaces
- Edges are edges!

2-D shapes
- Polygons have all straight sides.
- Regular polygons have sides all the same length.
- Parallel lines never meet – think of a train track!
- Perpendicular lines make a right angle.

Triangles
- An isosceles triangle has TWO EQUAL SIDES AND TWO EQUAL ANGLES. Picture an isosceles triangle as an arrow! A scalene triangle has THREE SIDES OF DIFFERENT LENGTHS and THREE ANGLES OF DIFFERENT SIZES. When picturing a scalene triangle, think of scaling a mountain that has an easy way up or a more difficult side to climb!

Symmetries
- When drawing reflections, remember to keep the correct distance from the mirror line.
- Remember, rotational symmetry is just working out how many ways the shape can fit EXACTLY on top of itself.

Angles
- Acute angle is between 0 and 89°
- Right angle = 90°
- Obtuse angle is between 91 and 179°
- Straight line = 180°
- Reflex angle is between 181 and 359°

Coordinates
- Always read ALONG the x axis and then UP the y axis.
- Always write (x) before (y), i.e. (x, y).

Measuring

Measuring weight and capacity
- 1000 grams = 1 kilogram (1000 g = 1 kg)
- 1000 kilograms = 1 ton (1000 kg = 1 ton)
- 1000 millilitres = 1 litre (1000 ml = 1 l)

Estimating measures
- Milli = very small
- Centi = small
- Kilo = big

Perimeter
- Perimeter is the distance all the way round the edge of a shape.

Area
- Area is the space covered up by the shape.
- Count the squares and remember area is always measured in units squared (cm^2, mm^2, m^2).

Reading scales
- CAREFULLY work out what each mark on the scale is worth.

Handling data

Pictograms
- With pictograms **picture = number**

  e.g. = 20 ice creams = 10 ice creams

Mean, median, range and mode
- Mean = sum of all values divided by number of values
- Median = middle number in sequence (always write down in order first)
- Range = difference between highest and lowest number
- Mode = most common value

Charts and graphs
- Be careful and accurate. Use a sharp pencil.
- Pie charts are good for percentages, fractions or decimals.

Using and applying mathematics

Simple formulae
- Talk through the formula in your head. It will make it easier.

Number patterns
- Check the difference between the numbers to find the pattern.

Estimating
- When rounding, remember 5 goes up! 6.785 rounds up to 6.79.

Answers

Page 11 – Decimal notation and negative numbers

1) 8 pounds, 26 pence 2) 56 pounds, 40 pence 3) 28 pounds, 4 pence
4) 780 pounds, 75 pence 5) 712 pounds, 97 pence

(a) is colder

Page 12 – Fractions

$\frac{6}{8}$ circled; $\frac{2}{8}$ not circled
Answers will vary e.g. $\frac{2}{8} = \frac{1}{4}$; $\frac{1}{3} = \frac{2}{6}$.

Page 13 – 2, 3, 4, 5 and 10 times tables

1) 2   2) 7   3) 70   4) 9   5) 5
6) 14   7) 8   8) 80   9) 6   10) 32
11) 5   12) 5   13) 6   14) 1   15) 7

Page 14 – Subtraction

1) 309   2) 382   3) 259   4) 317   5) 264   6) 361

Page 15 – Classifying shapes

	Cone	Cylinder	Sphere	Cuboid	Triangular-based pyramid	Triangular prism
Number of faces	2	3	1	6	4	5
Number of edges	1	2	0	12	6	9
Number of vertices	1	0	0	8	4	6

Page 16 – Tables and lists

1) Thomas   2) 2   3) My Little T-Rex and Justin from Year 4

Page 17 – Bar charts and pictograms

1) tuna mayonnaise   2) 7   3) 18

Page 18 – Place value

1) a) $\frac{8}{100}$ b) 8   c) $\frac{8}{1000}$ d) $\frac{8}{100}$ e) 800

2) a) $3 + \frac{6}{10} + \frac{7}{100} + \frac{5}{1000}$ b) $40 + 5 + \frac{7}{100} + \frac{3}{1000}$ c) $60 + \frac{7}{1000}$

Page 19 – Place value

1) 5.66, 5.68, 5.86, 56.8, 58.6
2) 8.456, 8.546, 8.564, 8.645, 8.654
3) 4.7, 4.9, 7.3, 7.4, 7.5, 7.9
4) 3.36 km, 3.66 km, 3.663 km, 36.36 km, 36.6 km

Page 20 – Proportions of a whole

1) a) 23%   b) 81%   c) 10%
2) a) 77%   b) 19%   c) 90%

Page 21 – Important proportions

1) a) car   b) 40

Page 22 – Ratio and proportion

1) 4:3   2) $\frac{3}{7}$

Page 23 – Number relationships
1) 1, 2, 3, 4, 6, 8, 12, 24   2) 1, 5, 7, 35
3) 1, 7, 49   4) 1, 2, 4, 8, 16, 32, 64
Square numbers to 100 are: 1, 4, 9, 16, 25, 36, 49, 64, 81, 100

Page 24 – Checking your answers
1) 457 check 457 + 67 = 524   2) 40 check 40 × 4 = 160
3) 6987 check 6987 + 897 = 7884   4) 45 check 45 × 50 = 2250

1) 7557 Rough answer = 700 × 10 = 7000   2) 283 Rough answer 400 – 100 = 300
3) 26 Rough answer 460 ÷ 20 = 23

Page 25 – Checking your answers
1011 / In his first calculation, Billy put 112 instead of 12 into his calculator. 435 × 112 = 48,720

Page 26 – Addition
1) 9493   2) 16639   3) 10288   4) 8206

Page 27 – Subtraction
1) 1818   2) 5772   3) 5613   4) 6786

Page 28 – Adding and subtracting decimals
1) 14.81   2) 123.5 m   3) £19.52   4) 29.17   5) 6.05   6) 27.65 g

Page 29 – Multiplying by 10 and 100
1) 760   2) 100   3) 54,300   4) 800   5) 18,000   6) 65

Page 30 – Dividing by 10 and 100
1) 840   2) 10   3) 50   4) 100   5) 90   6) 70

Page 31 – Short multiplication
1) 1944   2) 5080   3) 4452   4) 5635   5) 3470   6) 3411

Page 32 – Short division
1) 338 r1   2) 177 r1   3) 153 r2   4) 158 r5

Page 33 – Angles
Order of angles: 30°, 56°, 100°, 134°, 170° – d), a), e), b), c)
a) 40°   b) 62°   c) 137°

Page 34 – 2-D shapes
Answers will vary

Page 35 – Properties of other 2-D shapes
Answers will vary

Page 36 – Moving 2-D shapes
a)
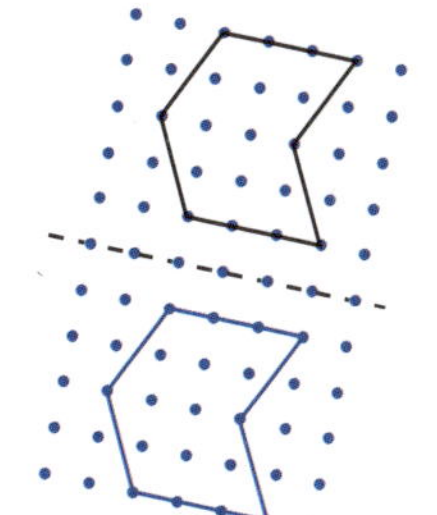
b)
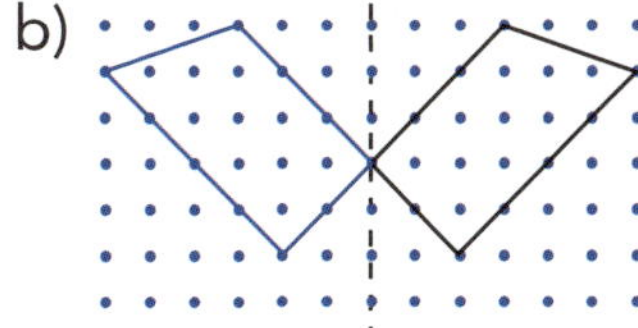

Page 37 – Moving 2-D shapes
1) a) 6   b) 4   c) 8

2) 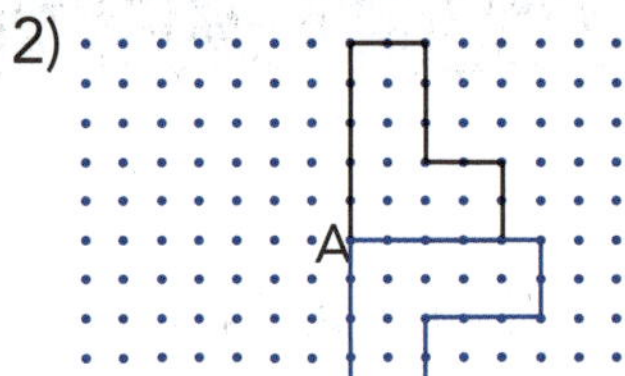

Page 38 – Using coordinates
1 a) (3, 2)   b) (3, 4)   c) (1, 5)
2 a) bumper cars b) Fun House

Page 39 – Using coordinates
The coordinates are (5, 2).

Page 40 – 3-D shapes
1) A – iii   2) 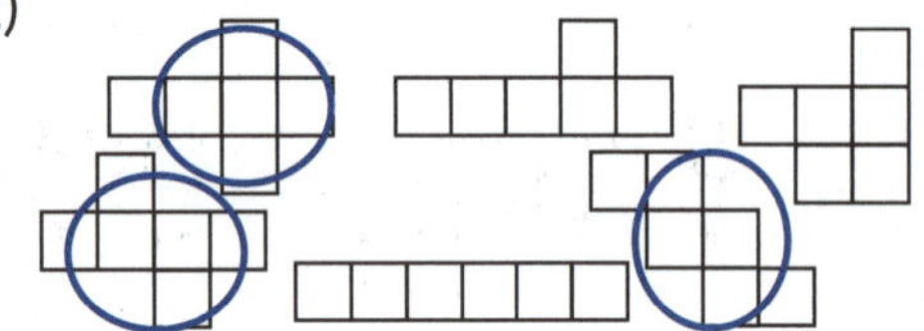
   B – ii
   C – iv
   D – v
   E – i

Page 41 – 3-D shapes
1) needs 8 blocks to complete the cuboid
2) needs 8 blocks to complete the cuboid

Page 42 – Measures
1) Your foot, DVD case   2) Glass of milk, can of cola   3) Scales
4) Ruler   5) Answers will vary. Use chart to check answers.

Page 43 – Reading scales
370 cm or 3.7 m

Page 44 – Perimeters of simple shapes
a) 13.2 cm   b) 18 cm

Page 46 – Grouping data
1) 2   2) 6   3) 6–10   4) 12   5) No they didn't

Page 48 – Line graphs
1) a) March   b) 1500   2) January and February   3) November
4) Description of event that would explain the increase (e.g. it was the summer holidays; there was a championship; they had a special offer/let people in free)
5) 3400 (allow 3350–3450 inclusive)

Page 49 – Line graphs
1) 5   2) Wednesday and Thursday
3) a) upwards/increasing/getting higher   b) Friday

Page 50 – Finding the range
Range = 5881 km

Page 51 – Finding the mode
Mode = 13

Page 52 – Number patterns
1) 20, 32. Rule is 'add 6'.
2) 6, 3. Rule is 'subtract 3'.
3) 57, 120, 141. Rule is 'add 21'.